To Jim [illegible]

I hope that you'll apply these insights to your life.

All the best!

[illegible signature]

Creative Leadership

Kenyon R. Baird, PhD

Published by R.C. Law & Co., Inc.
579 South State College Blvd.
Fullerton, CA 92631

Printed in the United States of America
ISBN 0-939925-62-1

ACKNOWLEDGEMENTS

Solomon suggested quite strongly that the making of books can be a wearisome task, and at times I have tended to agree with the man of incomparable wisdom. But then, again, Solomon was only writing what was to become the inspired Word. And with all of his worldly success and material gain, he didn't have the gaggle of friends surrounding him that I have enjoyed. After all, through the encouragement of my writing peers in the San Diego Christian Writers Guild which is guided along by Dr. "Woody" Wirt and so many others, I have enjoyed in some instances weekly input and invaluable constructive criticism from caring and knowledgeable fellow writers. Helen Des Ermia and Marian Packer are foremost in this group.

I would be remiss if I did not give appreciative mention to all of the graduate and undergraduate students which I have had the privilege of sharing the contents of these ideas for their shaping and polishing of thoughts which became useful. Only the reader will be able to determine if that interaction went far enough.

I wish to express my deep appreciation to Arlene Winters for rescuing me from my computer illiteracy, providing the skills necessary for unclogging the processes of expression. Dr. Glenn Balch has been a constant source of "can do" uplifting whose involvement provided the ultimate publishing contract with Robert C. Law who, in turn, has evidenced continuing patience, friendship and counsel to create the final product.

And finally, my ultimate gratitude is for my wife, Mary Lou, for enduring both the clutter and fascination of this kind of task. Solomon should have been so fortunate.

CONTENTS

Foreword i

Chapter 1
Changing Porcupines into Teddybears 3

Chapter 2
Maturity: The Goal of Leadership 16

Chapter 3
The Building Blocks of Personality 30

Chapter 4
Seeking Power Without God: The Authoritarian Syndrome 47

Chapter 5
Paradigms … Shifting and Otherwise 65

Chapter 6
The Polytrophic Leadership Continuum Model 73

Chapter 7
The Polytroph and Organizational Growth 85

Chapter 8
Leader Sins: Quarrels, Conflict, Alienation, Divided Houses 97

Chapter 9
Introduction to the System Approach Contract (SAC) 109

Chapter 10
SAC: Polytrophic Tool Without Peer 120

Chapter 11
If You Love Me … Feed My Lambs, Shepherd My Sheep, and Feed My Sheep! 140

LEADERNOTES

Sally and Organizational Axiotherapy 1

Good Listening Posture, Philadelphia Style! 14

This is Moses! 29

Wimpier and Weaker 45

Dictatorata 46

Master of the Second Guess 62

Status, Power and Control: South of the Border 82

Leadership and the Local Church 94

Dream Machines: Broken and Otherwise 107

Lateral Thinking 119

FOREWORD

There is no doubt about it! Mature people need solid food to carry out their manifold tasks. They need some potent nutrition that will serve them when spiritual energy demands are critical. What follows in this study is definitely not Pablum! And it is offered in the confidence that those who are genuinely interested in doing something about the problems in the contemporary church will glean an understanding of some of the essential dynamics that shaped us, and the strategic decisions available to every believer who wants to rekindle the flames of incendiary fellowship among Christians today.

> *We have much to explain about this, but it is hard to explain because you are slow to learn. In fact, though by this time you ought to be teachers, you need someone to teach you the elementary truths of God's word all over again. You need milk, not solid food. Anyone who lives on milk, still being an infant, is not acquainted with the teaching about righteousness. But solid food is for the mature, who by constant use have trained themselves to distinguish good from evil.*
>
> *Therefore let us leave the elementary teachings about Christ and go on to maturity....*

> *Land that drinks in the rain often falling on it and that produces a crop useful to those for whom it is farmed receives the blessing of God. But land that produces thorns and thistles is worthless and is in danger of being cursed. In the end it will be burned.*
>
> *Even though we speak like this, dear friends, we are confident of better things in your case—things that accompany salvation. God is not unjust; he will not forget your work and the love you have shown him as you have helped his people and continue to help them. We want each of you to show this same diligence to the very end, in order to make your hope sure. We do not want you to become lazy, but to imitate those who through faith and patience inherit what has been promised.* —Hebrews 5:11-6:1, 6:7-12.

This is a book for leaders about leadership. It explores Biblical dimensions in ways that have not been presented before, and does not shrink back from identifying some of the sins and pitfalls of leaders in its attempt to provide a Biblical basis for building people and the Christian church, including all of its para-church spin-offs. The author offers no apologies for the truths of God's word and its ability to penetrate to the soul and spirit, judging the thoughts and attitudes of the heart. (Heb.4:12) Believers involved in other temporal leadership pursuits will also find ready applications of these Biblical insights to their arenas of responsibility.

This book is written for those who aspire to do God's will in a Biblical fashion. It is for those whose minds have been trained by constant use to distinguish between good and evil. (Heb. 5:11-14) Thus it is offered to those who recognize their accountability and want to become responsible stewards in their roles as leaders. It depicts some basic principles that must be examined if we are to make the best decisions in that regard, decisions which carry serious consequences.

It has been said that Christians are "applied scientists." If that is the case, then Christian Leadership is the all-time applied science. What you are is what you get. You had better get all that the Lord has to give to you in your understanding of His truth as it applies to your life, because you will be held responsible for what you do with your influence on that day when you stand before Him. It is simply another reality and practical example of the Parable of the Talents.

Our "influence," or role as leaders, may profoundly impact those around us. How, when, where, and why it is employed is of critical import. It is not so much a matter of how much leadership talent we have, but how we apply it. This is stewardship.

God richly establishes each life, and each person as a resident manager of His domain. His commitment is to be with us always. He invites us to learn of Him. We enjoy nurturing experiences together. He restores the soul. Refurbishes our lives. He provides whatever is needed.

But does He make any request in return? Is there a hook in the eternal plan? Only in the sense that God knows our nature and what is good for us. Jesus reduced it all to two simple requirements: "Love the Lord with all your heart, soul and mind; and your neighbor as yourself." and, "Love one another." This, then, is the foundation of our appointment as resident managers, and the basis by which we recognize our responsibility to lead in love.

The Bible uses the term "stewardship" and carries with it a sense of accountability. But if the relationship between the child of God and the Father is kept healthy, this accounting becomes something between the child who brings home his artwork for parental approval and blessing, and the mature and hardened quarterback who strategizes with his coach in the middle of the conflict. There is a confident assurance, the close cooperation of working together, yet the inability to know exactly what the next events may lead to.

There is the sense of the ultimate accountability, for Paul wrote, "we must all appear before the judgement seat of Christ, that each one may receive what is due him for the things done while in the body, whether good or bad." This is not to be confused with the judgements about our sin. That was taken care of at Calvary. This has to do with our stewardship. It is concerned with what we have done with our lives after acquiring God's free gift of salvation and everything that comes with it. It is a final accounting of our resident managers ledgers. The issue really comes down to whether we have loved as Jesus loves us. Whether we have communicated clearly his love and truth as indicative of our own reception and reliance on that love and truth in our own lives. It has to do with our influence. It has to do with our leadership. I'm certain that there will be deep, deep, joy mingled with recurring tears of utter regret.

Let us take a peek at how our influence as Christian leaders might be working. Suppose, for the sake of example, that an individual's spiritual influences begin with a heritage of strict hyper-Calvinistic teaching, with its determinism that can become an alternative for the deep compassion which agape love demands. (I am citing that posture which suggests that God has already made up His mind about who will be judged as righteous and thereby redeemed, and who will be condemned, etc., which sometimes leads to the position that we as Christians carry out the business of communicating the Gospel solely out of rigid obedience to the Lord, with less than a deep compassion for the souls of men.)

Add to this an emotional inflexibility born of ultra-conservative values, perhaps an aloofness of Victorian prudery emanating from a denominational warping of the scriptures. Then maybe the person is the product of a home devoid of the rich, gracious, commitment of agape love that instills a relationship which goes beyond behaviors, the kind of love that is communicated by the attitude, "No matter what mistakes you may make, what choices you select, you are always our son, our daughter, and we love you, and we will always stand by you."

These may become some of the building blocks of personality, shaped through "spiritual" involvements, but lacking a correct understanding and application of the scriptures, leading to stunting and warping of spiritual development.

Perhaps there has not been the modeling of agape love in the life of the believer, the sacrificial commitment which performs even when one doesn't feel like it, or would rather be doing something else, or provides the greater payoff to another, or suffers for what is right. Devoid of such roles in their own spiritual development, a person can chose to become less of a lover, squandering opportunities to give by extracting for himself additional affection from others. Such a person may choose to use, take, and get in situations ripe for giving, serving, loving.

Then, of course, there exists the one big bomb of human spiritual arrestment, detonated within many aspiring and accomplished leaders:

the idolatry of the leadership office itself.

Assignments can easily be rationalized. "He needs the experience!" In the military there is the pregnant concept which is reduced to "RHIP." It means that Rank Has Its Privileges! Boot camp very effectively drums this principle home. For raw recruits it is an extremely traumatic period of indoctrination, learning to become obedient to another source of influence other than one's own sense of direction.

The problem also looms in Christendom whenever the leader begins to take himself too seriously in the notion that as God's emissary, he has God's privileges. After all, he speaks for God, makes strategic decisions on God's behalf, appears unaccountable to others (just like God), etc.

Surely there is greater freedom in the position of **leader** than there is in **follower.** Perks abound. Distasteful task? Delegate it to someone considered inferior.

He has the authority and may exercise the opportunity to evade the issue. Difficult task laden with possible no-win situations? The possibility of undermined status? Erosion of power? Loss of control? Better to sidestep that one! Perhaps one can use the executive privilege of simply naming a problem rather than solving it!

One pastor poorly handled a conflict which arose in a local church, on the verge of splitting over the issue of glossolalia or "speaking in tongues," by simply labelling the problem and the many lives affected as a "crisis of identity" for the church. I have always wondered whether he really believed that or was forced to that description because he could not possibly see the alternatives of loving confrontation, collaboration, integration, and eventually consensus. His choice to label the conflict in that manner concluded the conflict by making the split an actuality.

Given RHIP, it is not difficult to understand how Christian leaders may fall head over heels, infatuated with the office of leadership, and lose sight of their first love, the One who created the office, the One who is to be served ultimately by the office. It becomes a rather pure form of idolatry. But the consequences of this incidence are usually devastating.

I believe that there will be some frightening accountability when some of our revered leaders in contemporary Christendom stand before the throne of God and display the fruit of their stewardship. I fear that while they may believe that they have accomplished great things for God, they will be brought up short by the existence of many wounded brothers and sisters in Christ whom they maligned, trampled, used, and abused in their quest for getting the job done. Compared to "what might have been" had they chosen a leadership infused with love, their stewardship will appear quite shoddy.

The goal of this book is to provide the dynamics of nurturing relationships that will reduce the pain which Christians inflict upon each other and increase their ability to help others mature into capable leaders within the church and society.

As you may have sensed, this book about leadership provides a basis of human interaction and influence based on the New Testament principles of Agape love. It will provide a model displaying concepts and dynamics that occur if a person chooses to live a life reflecting the redemptive love of God in all areas of his stewardship of influence. The strong bias inherent in the book is that these principles and dynamics are absolutely essential to our ultimate stewardship before God, and if ignored, will tremendously undermine our effectiveness in all areas of our lives. If these truths are implemented through rational decision-making by contemporary leaders, the benefits of the fruit of the Spirit will enhance every person and group who in this manner follows the Lord Jesus in love.

This book also sets forth some ideas, principles, and dynamic leadership truths that have heretofore not been written. There are many reasons for this, not because the truths have not been available, but perhaps because the popular view of leadership generally has to do with commandeering a situation and plowing through the myriad of obstacles within the path of getting the job accomplished. While I can readily appreciate, and shall address, the necessity of task facilitation, getting the job done is only one side of the coin. Developing people, which remains the other side of leadership, unfortunately remains some sort of ancillary benefit in many leader's perspective. Too frequently groups and formal organizations have been so concerned about tasks that they have overlooked the responsibility of nurturing their most important resources; people. **A deadly delusion in business today is that capital, physical resources, and technology are valued more highly than the people who manage them.** For believers, the organizational church, Christian managers and organizations alike, the challenge continues to be one of blending the two responsibilities of leadership together. The TASK is developing PEOPLE to maturity!

One final introductory thought. The Lord has given us a mind, in fact, when we become His child he equips us with the "mind of Christ." There is every reason to believe that this faculty also is to be exercised. As a result, I expect that as you read these pages you will examine, comprehend, reason, evaluate, and make relevant decisions about yourself and your ability to love and serve others. In short, you will need to think. This is not a bowl full of Pablum, mush for the toothlessly immature. Remember that the author of the Hebrews wrote,

> *Anyone who lives on milk, being still an infant, is not acquainted with the teachings about righteousness. But solid food is for the mature, who by constant use have trained themselves to distinguish good from evil.* (5:13,14.)

James also advised,

> *If any of you lacks wisdom, he should ask God, who gives generously to all without finding fault, and it will be given to him.* (1:5)

May the Lord meet you in these pages as you examine His will for you regarding this most keenly important dimension of your life.

Kenyon R. Baird, PhD
Vista, California; 1990

SALLY AND ORGANIZATIONAL AXIOTHERAPY

"But she'll die if you don't take her home with you!" the little girl wailed on the sidewalk just outside of the pizza parlor.

"She'll get run over by a car if you don't take her!"

Sally has turned out to be a wailer just like the sobbing girl who promoted her adoption. A plain old three-colored urchin when we took her in, she even then had that deranged "meow." As she got bigger, Sally was pretty much tolerated with her incessant feline noise, and soon she went through the flip-around stage with the neighborhood runabouts. Then she developed those funny bulges that revealed her indiscretions, and started to sag in the middle.

One morning, as we all were hurrying to get to work, Sally started contracting, the wail even more plaintive. We arranged the maternity room, a cardboard box complete with well worn bath towel, and went to our appointed responsibilities. Upon returning in the evening, poor Sally was weak and dazed, but the bulges remained.

At the emergency meeting of the Family Finance Forum, it was determined that the needy "mother" was to be the recipient of financial aid for possible Caesarean section, to be expedited immediately. (After all, what's a couple of hundred dollars at such a pregnant moment!)

The vet discovered that the cat's uterus was blocked by an inadvertently ponderous and lifeless fetus. Sally would not have made it without incisive outside intervention.

But here was life! Perfectly formed and awaiting a timely birth. But blocked! Unable to come forth normally. Even Sally, the prime mover, nearly an occlusionary casualty. So much like so many situations in the human dimensions. Meaning, purpose, fulfillment, enthusiastic excitement, the *joie de vivre*, so often bottlenecked by thinking, attitudes, and values that are devoid of the life-giving truths of God's love in action. And the same holds true for organizations, including the local church. Many are corked, not able to bring authentic life to individuals or into their surrounding communities because of internal conflicts and pressures.

Incisive outside intervention! That's what it took for Sally to continue life. But the intervener had to be a skilled professional who didn't shrink before the task at hand. A pro is really someone who has skills, knowledge, and abilities honed and practiced so that when called upon in critical situations the difficult task can be accomplished with confidence. We still need healers for the needy, for individuals and for organizations.

Thankfully, a growing number of leaders now exist who have paid the price to acquire the necessary professionality to be competent organizational healers. Therapists. Consultants. Christian behavioral scientists. Men of science and men of the Word of God. Problem-solvers. People-oriented facilitators. Skilled in identifying values, prioritizing them, and when called upon, highly capable of sensitively inlaying the highest values for individuals, groups, and organizations. The jargon term "Organizational Axiotherapists" aptly describes a fresh discipline made up of applied scholars laboring in the field of the therapy of values. Some are called from more common forms of ministry, some from the ranks of Christian higher education, some from careers in secular business; all have a heart for God, and for the bride of Christ: the contemporary church. God bless every one of them.

Sally? She proved to be a survivor. Her two living kittens haven't been accepted by an adoption agency yet. Actually, the little Tom is really pretty cute, kind of resembles that fellow who lives over the backyard fence. But the little three-colored female is definitely scheduled for adoption promotion ... she should be old enough in about three days. She seems to have this wail....

CHAPTER ONE

Changing Porcupines into Teddybears

The PhD degree in clinical psychology was a lockstep program all the way at the state university. These were the required courses, offered in this sequence, in this time frame, and to obtain the degree, I knew that I couldn't miss a step. One probable breather was "Advanced Group Dynamics," which promised on the surface to be something that I could whiz through. I had many leadership experiences, and felt very comfortable in my handling of group interactions. I even took some undergraduate coursework in group dynamics which proved to be memorable. And ... I was a leader.

After all, I was elected captain and played quarterback on the college football team. I'd had four years of pro football, and now accepted the challenge of professional golf. I knew how to take command of a situation. I took pride in my natural gifts and knew how to work hard. I could make the commitment to get the job done. And both at the college level and in the pros we won the championship. My athletic role always seemed to open up other influential roles in church, civic groups, and business. And here at State, I was one of the few people to get accepted into a PhD program straight from the BA degree.

The professor was a rather attractive blond, with warm brown eyes that seemed to both penetrate and include as they swept the class. In addition to reading the normal texts and final exams, there was to be a group project which would also impact the grade. The large class of over one hundred twenty students was divided into four groups and funneled to their separate meeting places.

After a seemingly short period of time together, I was elected chairman pretty much by general consensus, and discussions centered on what sort of topic we should focus as our group project. One young lady made it pointedly clear that she was teaching full time, and could not be expected to put in any outside time other than that which was allotted during regular class hours. Quite a few others said they were in the same boat.

I quickly decided to work with those shakers and movers who were willing to do "something significant" as a class project. We'd blow the mind of the professor by accomplishing something substantial in the short time available for the project. I sensed an inner core numbering about seven of those who really wanted to do something, and felt that the others were just going to go along for the ride no matter what we did. We developed a plan for a complex learning study using nonsense syllables, based on the interests of Irving, who had become my lieutenant. Overly concerned Sylvia offered her house for the additional nights we had to gather for work, and Florence, long estranged from her husband and having ample free time, finally became the fourth member of the workers who would end up getting the project done.

And we brought it in on time, made the presentation, and kicked back in that earned confidence of a job pretty well done , considering the circumstances. After all, almost all of the larger group were simply not available for the task, so we did it ourselves. It was a shame that they might get the same grade as those of us who did all of the work. Oh well, that's human nature!

I couldn't believe my grade! I felt like I got hit over the head with a shovel. I was dumbfounded!

I stormed into the professor's office with my nose entirely pronged in an unusual vector. It was definitely out of shape. Didn't she know how I had to take the responsibility for the whole blasted group? ... and with perseverance and sacrifice of MY time, make that stupid project successful?

She read my body language, my anger, my response to this incredible atrocity, looked me square in the eye and firmly spoke,

"Baird, sit down. I've been meaning to talk to you."

She wasn't very big, but she spoke with a calm and commanding tone as she began to level me.

"You dummy! The group gave you its authority to lead ... and you simply just took it and went your merry way. You never gave it back to them! I've seen your kind before, and I wonder if you'll ever learn! I got a bunch of evaluations from the group about you and they were all pretty mad, really disgusted with you."

Could I have fumbled?

SO WHAT IS "LEADERSHIP"?

Leadership is an omnibus term that lies open for investment of meaning by any who use the concept. Leadership is something akin to belly buttons; everyone is involved with the phenomenon. Everyone has influence, used either negatively or positively. And leadership, in its broadest sense, is synonymous with influence. This notion is like the first principle set forth in the typical beginning college course, Philosophy 101, which indicated that all people are philosophers. That is, for example, they have ideas and thoughts about the nature of reality, make judgements about the relative values of a variety of concerns, generate conclusions about human nature, perform on the basis of some understanding about how humans think, and express interest in the ultimate meaning of life in general. And just as we are all philosophers, so are we all leaders. It is not a matter of whether or not we will choose to become leaders, a case of determining if we will influence others by what we think, say, or do. The concept of being a "born leader" is extremely freighted with conflicting discussions. We **have** this capacity. It comes with life. The issue concerns what we choose to do with our influence. The challenge is to learn how to become a good steward of this responsibility, a good manager of the asset which is dropped in our laps.

Just like other gifts which are bestowed upon us, we may refuse to recognize its existence, let it lie dormant, ignore its possibilities, squander it upon ourselves, or develop it to its pinnacle so that both we and others benefit from its gracious exercise. Stewardship can become a frightening thing. An aspect of maturity is to take responsibility for one's behaviors and the consequences of our actions. It is understandable that many attempt to take another, easier route in life. But ultimately, God holds us accountable.

Realizing this, it logically follows that our influence, or leadership capacity, is exercised in any number of ways, never in a vacuum, but in relationship. Some use their influence destructively, causing pain and harm; a display of negative influence. Others use their leadership to build. John's gospel contains the profound comparative principle from the Lord Jesus, "The thief comes only to steal and kill and destroy; I have come that they may have life, and have it abundantly." (John 10:10)

Looking at leadership this way probably contradicts notions that most people have when they think of leadership, typically focusing on the idea of autocratic leadership, Rambo I, II, III and IV! For these people, a leader only provides pointed direction, bidding others to do as he wills usually by the force of his personality or example. But there is much more to leadership. Our relationships, our influence, our leadership, all are to be exercised circumspectly if we are to be the kind of persons who represent the body of Christ winsomely. And we must become builders of others. That is what the Lord expects from his people. In talking about leadership we are also talking about the stewardship of our time and talent. This realization comes to all believers who understand that the whole of life ultimately falls under the lordship of our Creator-Redeemer.

But leadership takes many forms, as many forms as there are personalities. Each person adopts a style of leadership in the same way that he develops what may be referred to as a style of personality; one shaped by heredity, environment, other conditions and choices. Most important: we **choose** to become the kinds of influencers which we are. Our style of leadership can be modified once we understand the consequences of our decisions.

There is much written about personality styles as an attempt to understand human behavior. I really like the title of the recent book *The Delicate Art of Dancing With Porcupines,* subtitled, "Learning To

Appreciate The Finer Points of Others." What is being said suggests that you identify your personality style and learn how to make it work for you. A great deal of management theory parallels the same notion of learning what your style of management or leadership may be, then finding the best application, or organizational environment, for its exercise. In Christian applications, it is even suggested that this "style" is God given, rather static, and reasonably unchangeable.

Do I have news for you!

The GOOD NEWS, or gospel, is all about how God **changes** lives. His record of taking inconsequential people and making them magnificent persons of leadership and influence billboards throughout the Word of God. The good news is that you do not have to be the person you are; you can be born again, regrown, and matured into the person God truly can use in the contemporary world. Part of the good news is that God WILL change you. You will begin to love just the same way he has loved you. He will develop capacities you never dreamed could exist anywhere, let alone in you.

Sure, God will use the strengths of personality that have been shaped through heredity, environment, specific conditioning, and your past choices. But He will build in new dimensions, new qualities, new attitudes, foster the motivation and development of new abilities and new skills. If you were to reconstruct a damaged automobile, you would obtain new replacement parts, upgrade by installing the latest technology, and make it absolutely roadworthy. You probably would not attempt to change a Honda into a Mercedes, but you would find that your new Honda Acura performs every function as well as a Mercedes. Anyway, at that stage you would not care about mere brand names anymore. You would be too busy with your travels, knowing that you have honest and reliable transport to get where you are supposed to be going, doing what you are supposed to do.

Using the same analogy of reworking an automobile, a basic consideration for restoration following wear, tear, and accidents, is to make sure the frame is straight. Everything is going to be attached to the frame, and if it isn't aligned properly, everything that is assembled on it is going to be out of whack. It is similar to a foundation. It has to be firm, level, and straight.

As a behavioral scientist, let me be quick to affirm that the context of that which follows has as its framework, its foundation, its basis, the Word of God. The Bible remains the authoritative source for understanding human behavior. Used as a map, I have concluded from years of experience that, as the supremely appropriate guide for applying knowledge, the Bible bestows wisdom on those who follow its revelations. I make no efforts to defend its truths, merely take them at face value and attempt to apply them to the best of my ability in the contemporary world.

Then what of the pronouncements of the behavioral sciences? First, I recognize that scholars in the broad fields of psychology, sociology, anthropology, education, communication, management and organizational behavior have many wholesome contributions to make. I have attempted to take into consideration their findings whenever feasible. But I am also sensitive to the fact that many principles from these fields are founded on certain basic presuppositions and tenets that ought themselves to be examined in the light of biblical revelation. Somewhere along the pathway of gathering my own education I became aware of the notion that it was no longer the Bible that has to pass scrutiny. The Bible became a dependable fountainhead for learning, but the other voices were suspect. It became continually reaffirmed that those who left God out of the equation were building on a framework that was tragically misaligned. Resultantly, I use the behavioral sciences, its concepts, language, and findings, as a means of illustrating biblical truth. It seems far better to work with enduring revealed truth than with the next deduction from scientific methodology that, while providing more enlightenment when correctly understood and handled, still represents infinitesimal steps in the gathering of data.

Ultimately, it takes more than mere facts to bring meaning and purpose to life. It takes searing, unalloyed truth, intertwined with values rightly aligned with God's word, to generate lives that are significant, worthwhile, and poignant. Part of that truth lies in the revelation that lives change dramatically whenever they are touched by the living and true God, the God of the Bible, the God of Moses, Abraham, and Jacob. The God of Peter, James, John and Paul. People with profoundly changed lives. I hope that you enhance your relationship with Him as a result of this study. If so, then your invigorated life will freshly affirm that He is still working on many levels in believers today.

But the discussion should prepare you to understand that there are certain concepts flushing from the behavioral sciences that Christians have swallowed as gospel. Some of these are constructs, models, or what scientists in education like to call a *paradigm.* The Leadership Continuum set forth in this study illustrates this device for learning. My concern for the deployment of this teaching technique is that many students confuse these conceptual overlays (as helpful as they may be in describing events and/or relationships) with the real-world events that they are trying to comprehend. The models are maps to describe the territory. They are not the territory. They are not inviolate. They only represent a certain level of description which leaves out an enormous amount of information whenever they are applied to real events, real territory, real people.

I become somewhat agitated when I examine writers who take something such as personality "style" and freight that concept with something as heavy and binding as to imply that God has given to each of us a "style" that shackles us for life, when in actuality, as we grow, we change. My understanding of the Bible leads me to believe that we are all different, all unique, and each person has a specific purpose or calling. While I too use the concept of "style" in discussions, it is only a figure of speech, certainly not revelation, certainly not an unchangeable facet of human personality cut from any biblical author.

A similar case in point which believers hotly contest from time to time lies in the issue of dispensationalism in the Bible. The concept represents an overlay of scripture that is "extra-biblical," and therefore not to be confused with revelation. That is, if you go to the original manuscripts there will be no evidence of Rev. C. I. Schoefield's writings. While many individuals grew up with a Schoefield Reference Bible, rich in the dispensational viewpoint, who would die a martyr's death today if required to do so on the basis of Schoefield's dispensationalism? Yes, I know, there are probably some who might be willing.

The problem stems from the fact that belief in and use of these models somehow grows until they, too, are canonized. At this point they cannot be changed. Then people begin to believe that the map and the territory is the same thing. And if you are a certain "type" of person made to be that way, then why bother to explore becoming anything different? Why bother to grow? It can easily become a cop-out! This error of logic flies rampantly in the face of God's love and purpose for all of His creation. It hinders growth in those redeemed whom God is in the process of changing into mature trophies of his grace.

Whenever an individual life is examined, all of the sweeping generalizations go out of the window. One of the facinating properties of the Word of God lies in the manner in which it changes all people to become more like Christ, whoever they were before they came to him. Yet each person retains his uniqueness. There is no spiritual cloning. There is no cookie-cutter conformity. The German language has a fittingly descriptive phrase, a "ding und zeich," a thing in itself; that which has no copy. This is where we all live, move, and have our being.

I am concerned with how applying God's word will change me! I am not overly keen about knowing that I fit into some statistical grouping that has certain characteristics, which under certain circumstances, with certain other attendant conditions, have been known to obtain another qualified set of results. I have to surely know what God says and how his truth works effectively here and now in my life. That is enough. Then if I choose to apply his word as an act of faith, He becomes my sufficiency. Only then can I begin to experience first hand that "exchanged life," where Christ lives in and through me. Compared to all other life-"styles," nothing can compare to His!

The ensuing discussion will indeed set forth a model. It describes which natural leadership styles work best with people who are at differing stages of human growth and development. But unlike other paradigms, it includes biblical principles indicative of how the mercies, grace and love of God are unleashed in relationships that are structured on biblical truths. As you might expect, some significant dynamics unfold which require the attention of every person who desires God's best for their world. As your understanding grows, your maturity increases, so your life will change, and your effectiveness will increase as a leader in the kingdom of God.

You can expect to mature beyond dancing with porcupines, and begin to feel the warm, individualized, nurturing love of the Holy Spirit. It's something like getting a hug from a warm, very special, great big teddybear.

* * *

I eventually picked up the fumble.

The ball felt pretty slippery at first, but I started to get a handle on it. I began to ask questions when I found myself in discussion groups. The kinds of questions that were open ended and could be fielded in any number of ways depending on the wave length of the people in the group. In Bible studies I discovered that I didn't have to set an agenda for the passage under consideration. All I did to help open it up was to ask what it meant to the group, and in the most facinating way, was captivated by the manner in which the Lord gently led the group in discovery and application of the Word to their lives. I didn't have to give structure to the process, only in an indirect sense, such as asking questions like, "What do you suppose God is communicating to us here?" "Why do you think this says what it says in this particular way?" "Are we missing anything else in this passage?"

It became fun to explore how others thought and felt by asking instead of telling or even suggesting. Sometimes, I found that others reciprocally welcomed my opinions, guidance and input and I was happy to share from my experience. But there was no pressure to HAVE TO persuade others. Certainly I knew what outcomes were in accordance with the Word of God, but I recognized that God in His infinite patience would reveal the truths of His word to those who were ready to act upon it. I began to realize that it was quite possible to "lead from behind." I HAD DISCOVERED A MOST POWERFUL PRINCIPLE OF GODLY LEADERSHIP: GOD DESIRES TO WORK THROUGH HIS ENTIRE BODY OF BELIEVERS! I COULD DEPEND ON THE HOLY SPIRIT TO INDWELL AND WORK IN HIS CHILDREN.

Soon after this realization, I was given another starting assignment.

My second pastorate started with a small cadre of mostly retirement-aged people who were trying to make a church grow out of a Sunday school. A desert community, many people came to enjoy winters in true snowbird fashion. They brought with them almost every theological stripe and bearing. Some were Lutherans back home. There were Plymouth Brethren. Assorted Baptists. Methodists. Pentecostals. Church of God. Anglicans. Presbyterians. Some attenders had a deep grasp of the Word; others were glaringly illiterate in spiritual matters. Some raised their hands and spoke in tongues, others were pretty well convinced that glossolalia was a phoney psychological phenomenon. Many didn't even notice what was going on, content with nominal passivity. But this was the only church in town.

The town was split socio-economically with a middle-class, gated, golf-course community smack in the middle of an older, windswept mixture of small, quite inexpensive houses. Sand blew everywhere. When midweek Bible studies were announced, I discovered that the people from the older part of town never ventured into the homes of those who lived at the golf course. Very few from the golf course homes made it to the homes outside of their compound.

My predecessor had become discouraged with these churchfolk, feeling that they were not really interested in pulling together. There were quite a few who had their own agendas for what this group should become. He concluded that he had better opportunities to do God's work at another larger, established church.

Over the next three and a half years, average attendance grew to over one hundred for Sunday worship. Sunday school grew, offering an elective schedule for a variety of interests. The new organ and piano enhanced the singing which became a trademark for the blossoming group. A new constitution was created and installed. Many came to a saving knowledge of Christ. The church completed a building program free of any debt. The community of believers bridged their social and economic differences and became an ongoing vibrant church institution increasingly capable of meeting the needs of the surrounding community. Since I moved from that church it has continued to grow, to build, to perform.

I think that I finally learned some lessons about fumbling and recovering. Among other things, I discovered that it was far better to be in the position of "handing off" to others who were not only skilled at

> carrying the ball, but even had the Lord's resources to create some very good game plans themselves. My stewardship of the pastoral office was blessed beyond my expectations. I tend to think that it was because I started to do things in accordance with the Lord's clear directives in the Word of loving as Christ loved. "By THIS all men will know that you are my disciples, if you love one another." (John 13:35)

But before we get too far in this study, let's look at what we mean by maturity.

GOOD LISTENING POSTURE, PHILADELPHIA STYLE!

At the end of the volatile sixties, I had a consulting opportunity to attempt to develop an inner-city group living home for dependent, pre-delinquent and delinquent youth in the Philadelphia ghetto. I finally convinced the predominantly white, suburban, leadergroup that, to hold any possibility for success, it was necessary for the staffing to be primarily black, inner-city residents, who shared a commitment to Jesus Christ.

Concurrently, Gordon Theological Seminary near Boston was in the process of merging with the Conwell Seminary group which had long enjoyed its role buttressing Temple University in downtown Philadelphia, thus becoming the present Gordon-Conwell Theological Seminary of Wenham, Massachusetts. Prior to merger discussions, Conwell had recruited an outstanding, though in some instances non-traditional faculty, in an attempt to respond to the problems that were wrenching the nation in terms of racial, economic, political, family and spiritual issues energized by ghetto violence and riots. The Philadelphia seminary was developing a core curriculum for dealing with the magnitude of the problem, and was headed by an erudite, sophisticated, scholar from Australia at the time. I decided that it would be beneficial to take some coursework, not only for the opportunities to contend with the ideas which were being offered in a sound evangelical context, but also to take advantage of interaction with such a distinguished assemblage of Christian thinkers.

In the course of my consulting responsibilities, I tracked down some of the black leaders of the inner-city churches and power groups, attempting to gather their support and backing for the youth-oriented project. The seminary's role and input became a topic of discussion, as well as the Anglican scholar who was the conspicuous president. One black leader voiced that the president's behavior was significant for a white man operating in the inner-city. He described it:

> His posture is admirable. He has one ear to the ground and he is listening, genuinely trying to react to the sounds that he hears. The only problem is, that he hears hoofbeats. But he doesn't know if it's the Calvary or the Indians coming!

CALVIN AND HOBBES By Bill Watterson

CHAPTER TWO

Maturity: The Goal of Leadership

It is a great pity that men and women forget that they have been children. Parents are apt to be foreigners to their sons and daughters. Maturity is the gate of Paradise which shuts behind us; and our memories are gradually weaned from the glories in which our nativity was cradled. —George William Curtis

"When I was a child, I talked like a child, I thought like a child, I reasoned like a child. When I became a man, I put childish ways behind me." —I Corinthians 13:11 [NIV]

Any instructor worth his salt will provide examinations as a normal part of any study. Examinations should be a learning process, a check point along the pathway of assimilating knowledge and learning to use it. Let us see how we shape up in some basic areas of human growth and development. It may be threatening to inspect fruit if the orchard is not yet ripe, or has had infestations of harmful agents. Yet feedback is essential to determine where we are if we are at all interested in getting to where we should be.

A DEVELOPMENTAL TEST

While working as a consultant with a major league baseball organization, I naturally encountered people of varying stripes of personality and stages of human development.

I used an illustration of maturity and wholeness that conveyed some simple truths, the DEVELOPMENTAL WHEEL OF LIFE. It became a useful tool for both self analysis and for providing a frame of reference to understand some dimensions about basic maturity.

Picture a wheel with six spokes coming from the inner hub to the rim. Place a scale of one to ten on each spoke so that the one is next to the hub and the ten is next to the rim.

Then label each spoke: physical development, social development, family development, financial development, mental and educational development, and spiritual development.

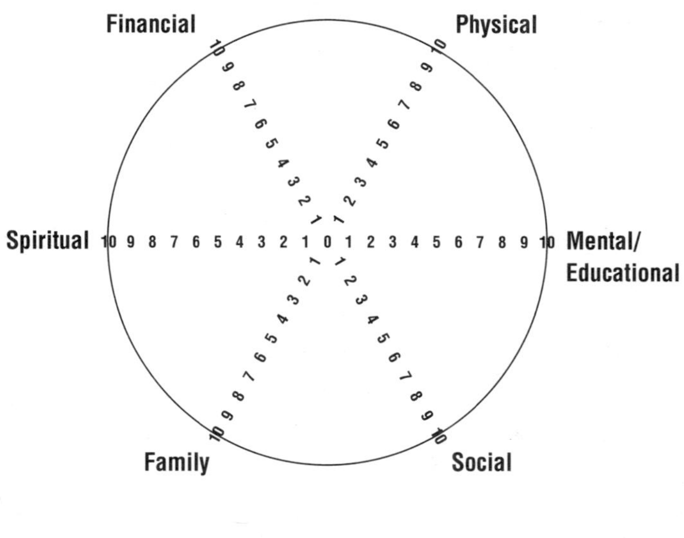

Then give yourself a self-graded test. Mark on each spoke where you believe you are in terms of your own development, on the scale of one-to-ten; ten being totally developed. Consider your age, experience, choices, and the world in which you function. Reflect on some of the following thoughts as you examine yourself:

Physical: What shape are you in at present? Are you overweight? Underweight? Can you do exercises easily? Could you run a 10K race tomorrow?

Are you robust? Or busted?

Social: Do you have a pool of close friends? Are you involved with a range of concerns in your church and community? Are you aware of issues affecting contemporary society; have you determined your convictions regarding them and chosen active involvement in their resolution? Are you sought out for advice by others? How would you measure your status?

Family: How are your relationships in your nuclear family? With Spouse? Parents? Children? Relatives? Are normal conflicts handled satisfactorily? Is there considerable room for improvement? Do you sense how you could make improvements? How do you evaluate your role and influence in your family?

Mental/Educational: Have you finished your formal education? Have you fallen short of what you thought you should accomplish? Are you aware of disciplines in which you are not knowledgeable? Do you know how to find information? Do you know how to discover resources? Are you a clear, logical thinker? To what levels have you developed your understanding of the world in which you live; its cultures, systems, peoples, and ideas.

Financial: What is your attitude towards money? Where do you place your understanding of money in your scale of values? How have you handled your financial affairs? Have you developed the skills, knowledge, and attitudes necessary for building personal financial independence? Are you a skilled investor? What is your approach towards philanthropy?

Spiritual: Does your spirituality reside as one facet of personality or does it permeate all of living? Have you been born twice? Do you experience a close walk with God? To what degree are you dependent upon the Lord? How does your relationship with God compare with biblical role models? Is there clarity in your choices and applications of values? Is the security of your faith evidenced by a deep sense of joy? Of peace? Of love? Are you excited by events that promise to change your life, knowing that God is in complete control?

Put a mark on each spoke where you think you are developmentally. Then connect the marks by drawing a straight line from spoke to spoke. Notice any flat spots on your wheel? Oblong and imbalanced wheels have been known to cause vibration, irritation, friction, and all sorts of crashes. Most times they give off a "lub-lub-lub" kind of noise as they motor through life, creating undue stress for both inhabitants and unsuspecting fellow passengers.

If this test indicates that you have significant room for growth, welcome to the human race! Do not be overly concerned. You are probably "normal." But, do not hesitate to think seriously about the person you could become with God's help and welcomed intervention. There is a profound principle penned by Paul, which offers both relief and excitement for growing persons;

> *For we are God's workmanship, created in Christ Jesus to do good works, which God prepared in advance for us to do.* (Eph.2:10)

We are a work of art which God is creating as he carries forth his sovereign purposes and plans.

MATURITY

It is normal for living things to grow through stages to adulthood and complete functionality. Caterpillars continue their mutations to become butterflies. As the *Fiddler on the Roof* song says, "Seedlings turn overnight to sunflowers, blossoming even as they grow." Advertising, a cultural reflection, showcases magnificent Clydesdale horses, muscles rippling, thundering over hills and streams as they capture the vitality of a fully adult creature. How sad by comparison is abnormality; stunted in growth, malformed in personality, fostering varieties of internal conflicts.

In Behavioral Science

An understanding of human development and its various implications has always been of interest to thinkers.

Some years ago, the brilliant psychologist and thinker Abraham Maslow grew disenchanted with the two predominate schools of thought which were in vogue in mid-twentieth century contemporary psychology. He was joined by voices; other psychologists, sociologists, anthropologists, educators, and management theorists, in what has since become billed as a movement in the behavioral sciences. The group reacted to the pervasive Freudian theory and practice that dominated psychology, education, jurisprudence, religion, art, literature, social philosophy, and even child-rearing.

Freud was a pioneer who attempted to solve the problems of those he termed mentally ill. Maslow criticized his studies principally on the basis of sampling error. He reasoned that if Freud primarily studied only the uptight, constricted, frustrated Prussian mind, laden with sexually freighted concerns, then his findings when applied to the whole of human enterprise was a rather spurious deduction.

Humorists have had fun with the so-called Freudian classical approach, complete with couch and note pad. One story shows the eminent psychiatrist counseling his patient who supposedly is concerned about his mental health. He asks the patient what he thinks about as he is confronted with the diagram of a triangle.

"Sex!" he admits.

"And what about this picture?" probes the doctor, as he shows him a diagram of a cube.

"Sex."

"And this?" showing now the form of a square.

"Sex."

"Well now," the psychoanalyst says, " I believe that I have diagnosed your problem, young man. You have a preoccupation with 'sex'!"

To which the patient responds, "My problem is it? You are the one showing me all the provocative pictures!"

The other psychological school of thought that Maslow addressed in his debunking efforts was the behaviorist. Where Freud was concerned with the inner workings of mental processes, John B. Watson and his followers relied on the outer or environmental influences on man, believing that human behavior results from habit formation in response to outside stimulation. The burden of proof to handle notions of freedom, justice, happiness, ethics, morals, and values led the behaviorist to conclude that these are only the result of associative learning.

Maslow discounted the behaviorist for the unreasonable deductive leaps of theoreticians who, upon experimenting with animal behavior and applying their findings to humans, concluded that man was merely another level of animal.

The best method of studying man, according to Maslow, was to examine the most outstanding examples of the species. Followers of Maslow's logic came to believe that there are values, or moral principles common to the entire human species, which can be confirmed by scientific investigation.

He found the old values, truth, goodness, and beauty, and some additional ones as well ... for instance, gaiety, justice and joy. "It looks as if there were a single ultimate value for mankind, a far goal toward which all men strive," he concluded.

This is called variously by different authors; self-actualization, self-realization, integration, psychological health, individuation, autonomy, creativity, productivity ... but they all agree that this amounts to realizing the potentialities of the person, i.e., becoming fully human, everything that the person can be.

In humans, according to Abraham Maslow, only 2% of the population make it to "actualization," his psychological term that describes mature manhood. Some contemporary thinkers, like the neophyte mountain climber who first comprehended Mt. Everest, tend to conclude "I'll never make it in this life!"

In Biblical Perspective

The biblical view, somewhat gentler, provides bright insightful word pictures illustrating the kind of nurturing relationships that foster growth and maturation. There is quite an impressive list of character traits and qualities given for people who are in the process of becoming full-grown examples of what it means to be totally alive, fully human, and mature: love, joy, peace, patience, kindness, goodness, faithfulness, gentleness, and self-control. These qualities issue from the spiritual dimensions of personhood, the highest measure of humanity.

Of all the qualities, the greatest is love, but the Bible identifies a particular kind of love called "agape." There is nothing quite like it anywhere else. Even its exercise in human dimensions implies a certain maturity inherent in the giver. The picture is of a tree that is mature, having the expected fruit, ripened and available, freely enjoyable for those who may need and desire them. Agape love is essentially a rational choice that we become capable of making when we consider the best interests of other persons. Its exercise implies that we have first had our own needs met in a personal relationship with God so that we are free to develop concern for someone else.

Both the writers of the gospels as well as the author of Hebrews, and James, and Paul make use of the concept of maturity in the Bible. You would expect that the good doctor Luke would include it in his many therapies, and he does as he recounts the parable of the sower. The story, given variously in the gospels, not only gives a parable, but the explanation of the parable which was reserved for the inner circle of those who were following Jesus. Luke's sensitive recollection of Jesus' explanation picked up another conclusion that Matthew, for instance, seems to have glossed over. It is quite typical of Luke, the loving physician, to depict things in a slightly different light.

You know the story. It begins in chapter eight of Luke's Gospel. Starting at verse eleven Jesus is explaining the parable:

> *This is the meaning of the parable: The seed is the word of God. Those along the path are the ones who hear, and then the devil comes and takes away the word from their hearts, so that they may not believe and be saved. Those on the rock are the one who receive the word with joy when they hear it, but in the time of testing they fall away. The seed that fell among thorns stands for those who hear, but as they go on their way they are choked by life's worries, riches and pleasures, and they do not MATURE. But the seed on good soil stands for those with a noble and good heart, who hear the word, retain it, and by persevering produce a crop.*

It's pretty simple. The concerns of fear, power, and pleasure can choke a person's growth towards maturity. Those that become mature produce a crop; there is visible fruit in and of their life.

James, the brother of Jesus, was a victim of all sorts of persecution which was typical of the early church. He was martyred in A.D. 62. Paul called him a pillar of the church, and he was a leader in the important council of Jerusalem (Acts 15:13). As his letter reflects, James had clear purpose and bearing. Martyrdom is not accidental. James' white hot logic stills sears our thinking today:

> *Consider it pure joy, my brothers, whenever you face trials of many kinds, because you know that the testing of your faith develops perseverance. Perseverance must finish its work so that you may be MATURE and complete, not lacking anything.* (James 1:2-4)

It appears that James' statement about maturity is based on the assumption that maturity has its own value. It is the reason for which God in his infinite wisdom allows his people to undergo hardships, and what James called "testing." Obviously, it is God's purpose for us to become mature.

The apostle Paul uses the term in a variety of circumstances. It should be noted, however, that the word in Greek is the noun "teleos," and generally translates in English as "perfect, as complete in all its parts; full-grown, of full age; and specially of the completeness of Christian character." In its verb form the word becomes, "To complete, to finish, as a course, or a race."

Please notice right here, the Christian life is not a sprint. It is more like a marathon. If you have just run into your own personal "wall," that agonizing stage in the race where your body craves the breath that it cannot momentarily obtain, your legs cramping and screaming at you; that place somewhat out of the starting blocks, but with the finish line nowhere in sight; hang in there, this is for you! These Biblical principles shout encouragement from the sidelines to everyone that runs the race. Biblical truth is always a breath of fresh air, always available in the most suffocating moments.

Paul, in his final greetings to the church at Colosse, includes his fellow leader Epaphras' prayer for them, "that you may stand firm in all the will of God, MATURE and fully assured." (Col.4:12) Picture these compassionate servant-leaders enjoying their role of catalyst for the development of others.

The writer of the letter to the Hebrews says that "solid food is for the MATURE, [those] who by constant use [of God's truth] have trained themselves to distinguish good from evil." Maturity is found to be anything but passive. The quality includes taking the initiative and responsibility for making things happen, particularly in one's own life. How welcome is the person who, sensing that something ought to be accomplished, digs in without hesitation or fanfare and does the appropriate thing! It also seems apparent, that the person who becomes mature, distinguishing between good and evil, is not operating from any sense of personal deficiency, and is therefore not prone to the manipulations of others.

The choicest use of the word is found in Paul's discussion in Ephesians 4:11ff. He talks about the various offices in the early church as "gifts," citing the offices of apostles, prophets, evangelists, pastors and teachers. These leaders are to

> *prepare God's people for works of service, so that the body of Christ may be built up until we all reach unity in the faith and in the knowledge of the Son of God and become MATURE, attaining to the whole measure of the fullness of Christ. Then we will no*

> *longer be infants, tossed back and forth by the waves, and blown here and there by every wind of teaching and by the cunning and craftiness of men in their deceitful scheming. Instead, speaking the truth in love, we will in all things grow up into him who is the Head, that is, Christ. From him the whole body, joined and held together by every supporting ligament, grows and builds itself up in love, as each part does its work.*

The greatest tragedy lies in the manner in which this passage has been largely ignored by those who have become leaders and officers in the contemporary church.

I mentioned above how the biblical view was somewhat gentler in its expectations of human functionality. Look again at the fourth chapter of Ephesians. Verse 16, as translated above in the New International Version (NIV), leaves something to be desired as it reads:

> *From him (Christ) the whole body, joined and held together by every supporting ligament, grows and builds itself up in love, as each part does its work.*

A closer rendering of the text gives:

> *[Christ] from whom the whole body, fitted together and connected by every resourcing joint (aphes), as measured by the energizing of each and every part, nurtures and builds itself up in love.*

This clearer translation of a somewhat difficult and complex text readily provides some startling principles:

1. When we become mature, we model Christ in our behavior.

Christ is the head of the church, and the head of each and every believer. We get our direction only from him. It is Christ who is the source and goal of our growth. To become fully mature is to become fully human, with the inborn Spirit of God totally dominating the rest of life's dimensions. The mature person makes the decision to turn his life over to the control of the Holy Spirit on a daily basis. This is what it means to grow up "into Christ," by far the most practical choice any person can make. When the Spirit controls a life, it begins to resemble Jesus' life, loving, and full of grace and truth. To perceive a model of human maturity, look carefully at the life of Jesus Christ.

2. Joints are an important part of a living body.

A proper biblical understanding of another believer is to appreciate that person as a resource; for you as an individual, to the local community of believers, and to the church universal. That other person has God's Spirit within him, is equipped with the mind of Christ, is washed with the selfsame blood of Christ as you, has been gifted by God, is so precious to the Lord Jesus that he died in his place, has also been personally called to a life of loving service, has extremely similar growth needs as you have, and has meaning, purpose, and fulfillment when resourcing and nurturing others. Sometimes that "resourcing" function is as simple as sharing how Christ has been operating in his life from a purely experiential viewpoint ... not preachy, not as the last word on an issue, but simply a testimonial voice that offers, "This is how the Lord has been working this out in my life." Transparently, the word of God says that my brothers and sisters in Christ are important, they are to be valued! They are not to be ignored nor manipulated for selfish concerns. These precious persons are to be loved.

3. Every joint is to be energized, working.

By measuring how much the "body parts" of the local church are "energized," i.e., how much each person is functioning or involved at any level, it is possible to determine how much an organization like the church is alive, healthy, and growing. There exists an old saw that says, "in any organization, 80% of the work is done by 20% of the people." This is probably true of many organizations—the very inept and sickly ones. Authentic building of people, groups, and organizations occurs when individuals believe and feel that they belong, they have a contribution to make, and that they and their contributions matter here, now, and in the future.

4. The joints, operating in love, nourish the body.

The "whole body," consisting of all those who have put their personal trust and faith in Christ, is nurtured and grows through the effective exercise of each "joint," that is, the relationships that each person has with each other person. While it is true that the ultimate source of power comes from the Lord, this passage indicates that He chooses to lubricate by the oil of his Spirit the parts of the body at the points of our interpersonal relationships. Our interface with each other becomes the force, the power, that nurtures the body when those relationships are functioning in agape love, the healthy and proper way. Conversely, whenever these basic interpersonal relationships are malfunctioning, the body relapses into stunted growth, ill health, festering sores, and eventual death.

5. Healthy parts, lovingly joined, produce growth.

To the degree that we join together appropriately, that is, in the bonds of God's agape love, we begin to discover what the Lord is doing in each of our lives, and it affirms his continued love for us, and his continuous working in and through us. This can become a deeply satisfying source of encouragement for all believers. We also discover that the Lord has created us all as tremendously unique individuals.

And , while he treats us all with love, we discover how strikingly different is that manifestation of divine love. One result of authentic fellowship in Christ is the personal liberation we enjoy when we begin to obtain a broader perspective of the whole economy of God. Not only does He accomplish His purposes in an endless variety of ways, but He doesn't always explain what He is doing in someone else's life or how He intends to do it. It kind of gives pause to the would-be god-players by giving the impression that the Lord is God, and for anyone else, it's OK to be merely human.

But there is an element of outrageous humor in the biblical map of supernatural human development. It is this.

God in his infinite wisdom has given all his children gifts. These are spiritual gifts, and they are bestowed similarly as the talents that we are given genetically. We don't do much to acquire them. They are "givens." And like the natural talents, nobody has all of them. Certainly there are one talent, two-talent, and thirteen-talent people in our populations, but hilariously, it almost seems that some individuals with the brightest shining gifts in one area are glaringly deficient in other areas. College campuses are notorious for harboring the types of immense intellects that somehow forget where they parked the car. Talk about God's sense of humor! He opted to make us that way. Why? So that only by (*aphes*) joining of ourselves to each other by love can we become fully functional.

He built into us the necessity of cooperation, not blaring independence. Just like the picture puzzle with intricately fitted pieces, we are to join to one another in Christian love so that we as individuals become enthusiastic about what God does through us collectively, until we willingly consent to modify our distinctiveness, becoming so much more than lonely individuals. Of course, those dynamics of losing your life and truly finding it again readily apply.

The word picture that Paul used was a familiar one in his day. The Greek word "aphes" literally means a joint, such as a joint of the body where two appendages unite. But the term also bears with it a connotation carried from its old classical usage of a log being united with flame so that in their joining they became flaming embers. Certainly the original nature of the ingredients change by this merger, but in changing their identity each acquired more dimensionality by assimilating the characteristics of the other entity. The word creates the picture of torching up a fire, blazing, warming, and in many instances, igniting others to action. The incendiary relationship endures as a timeless portrait of God's agape love.

Mature people. After all is said and done, what are they really like? As the Bible readily indicates, the mature person is someone who knows Christ as his personal Saviour. It would be impossible to be mature without being fully grown spiritually, and a person cannot become fully grown unless he is born again spiritually. When a person receives Christ, and the provision for his sin that Jesus alone freely gives, only then is he born from above—born again—born spiritually.

As a person grows in the Spirit, he will begin to bear fruit. *"The fruit of the Spirit is love, joy, peace, patience, kindness, goodness, faithfulness, gentleness and self-control"* (Gal.5:22). The mature person, then, will abundantly display these fruits or qualities in his life. They will impact all other dimensions of it.

There are obviously many other qualities inherent in the mature personality. Certainly, creativity flows from the freed-up mind, no longer guilt ridden. Mature people have the capacity for spontaneity, having confidence to do the appropriate thing and, while exhibiting self-control, know that as long as they act in love, whatever response they have will reflect genuineness and authenticity. They do not confront their world with a facade. What you see is what you get, but what you get reflects love.

Mature people want to be genuine craftsmen in their interactions with others in all kinds of relationships. They care greatly about the nature of their production, wanting it to reflect the best workmanship available, whether they offer goods or services. They want to do things with quality.

They have an inner-directedness, the gyroscope of the Holy Spirit influencing the direction of every thought and attitude. While they take into consideration what others may think, say, or do, they know that they are ultimately responsible for their behaviors, and choose to be guided by the Lord.

Mature persons polish communication skills which reflect their awareness of the world in which they live. They are in touch with their thinking, emotions, and choices. They develop a world-view; significantly evaluating the varieties of forces and systems at work in contemporary society. They can explain events in light of the Word of God. They complete complex tasks.

They tend to be assured in their bearing, relying on the Lord to guide them at every turn, but they are never smug. They recognize how dependent they have become on the Lord, and their awesome realization of their own human frailty whenever they attempt to live life in their own human strength rather than by God's enabling grace, has engendered a deep humility. Through their own history and relationship with God, they become sensitive to the plights of others.

In light of the tremendous forces in the world, mature people truly are God's workmanship!

THIS IS MOSES!

My wife and I frequently have provided care for children who have had difficult times, having them become prized members of the family if only on a temporary basis. Before being reunited with his mom, Israel, a robust eleven-year-old made good use of our trampoline. When new neighbors moved in across the street, their young boy's eyes lit up in rapt attention as my wife explained Israel's use of the trampoline to his mother. But his delight seemed to exceed any reasonable explanation. She finally understood his unbridled curiosity when the mother introduced her son, "This is Moses!"

CHAPTER THREE

The Building Blocks of Personality

An impeccable Englishman stood at an airline ticket counter as a pushy woman cut into line, slapped down her ticket and demanded an upgrade to first-class.

"Madame," the Englishman said, as he picked up her ticket and pressed it back into her hand, "first-class is not a boarding pass. It is a way of life."

Sometimes you cannot help but wonder how and where certain behaviors form. Frequently we only see the tip of the iceberg when observing human behavior. So much of personality is hidden from our view.

But what is "personality?" The term is a construct to describe three general areas of behavior; consistency, organization, and uniqueness. People who display intelligence in one situation usually can be seen behaving intelligently when confronting a variety of other situations. This type of consistency implies that certain behavioral characteristics of "personality" are predictable. The second area, organization, reflects that a person is not "merely a bundle of separate attributes tied together by a skin." If we observe the President of the United States, "we see long-term directions, overall goals, and aspirations—patterns of behavior in which some enduring attributes are subordinate to others."[1] In the third area, uniqueness, we note that no two people, not even identical twins, behave precisely the same way. Personality has to do with individual differences. A reasonable definition of personality, then, is the "unique organization of endearing attributes of the individual."

Values tend to form the foundation of a person's character and personality. We develop a value system, working like a subconscious mental filter, through which we sift the experiences we encounter in life and by which we make decisions. For each person it defines what is really important. It guides our choices and behavior, and defines integrity. Personalities may be enhanced by circumstances that reinforce values, or may be inhibited by circumstances inconsistent with those values. A person's value system defines the range of allowable choices and goals, and may provoke strong defensive behavior when challenged or attacked. Once the value system is formed, it tends to be entrenched in one's personality throughout a lifetime.

Luke gives the account of Simon the sorcerer in Acts 8:9ff. It seems that this man had developed a life style in Samaria based on magic which gave him considerable status, power, and control of other people. But when his followers responded to Phillip as he preached the good news of the kingdom of God and the name of Jesus Christ, they believed and were baptized, Simon along with them. "And he followed Phillip everywhere, astonished by the great signs and miracles he saw." The apostles in Jerusalem sent Peter and John to Samaria, and they placed their hands on the new believers who then received the Holy Spirit. Verse 18 reveals how entrenched was Simon's value system.

> *When Simon saw that the Spirit was given at the laying on of the apostles' hands, he offered them money and said, "Give me also this ability so that everyone on whom I lay my hands may receive the Holy Spirit."*
>
> *Peter answered: "May your money perish with you, because you thought you could buy the gift of God with money! You have no part or share in this ministry, because your heart is not right with God. Repent of this wickedness and pray to the Lord. Perhaps he will forgive you for having such a thought*

> *in your heart. For I see that you are full of bitterness and captive to sin."*

Simon's purpose for discipleship was to obtain personal influence over others by accumulating greater power. His value system maintained itself even in the face of God's truth and offer of salvation. Apparently, this filter caused him to remain insensitive to the gospel's redeeming powers for complete wholeness. It is interesting to note that in early Christian literature the "sorcerer," Simon Magus, is described as the arch-heretic of the church, and the "father" of gnostic teaching. He never responded positively to Peter's directive to repent. He never did change.

Value systems tend to exist in a hierarchy, with some held to be more important than others, offering the potential of value conflict. The parent who administers that old fashioned spanking to his child may really experience conflict when he says, "This is going to hurt me more than it does you!" His value of justice requires punishment. But realizing that he has become cast in a role as administrator of that justice, he becomes doubly sensitive to his values regarding his role of compassionate father, and the desire to continuously communicate his love. So he applies the "board of education to the seat of knowledge" and follows that choice with a hug, trusting that the offending child will receive the message that it was the child's behavior that has been dealt with. Dad still loves the child, but he doesn't approve of the behavior. The child is not the issue, it is his behavior that is the issue! Values upon values.

But where do values come from?

Dr. Morris Massey, professor of human behavior at the University of Colorado, has developed a reasonable thesis regarding the manner in which our value systems are shaped during our developmental years. His point of view entitled, "What You Are Is Where You Were When,"[2] indicates that we have prime periods of developmental life when complex programming or "imprinting" of our value systems occurs.

Most observers of human behavior have come to the conclusion that a child's first three to four years shape the personality and value system. During this period of INFANCY, a stage of development characterized by DEPENDENCY, a child observes the way things are and lays down a foundation of reality. He senses, "This is what a mommy is like, this is what a daddy is like, this is how a family works." For some, the conclusions of early childhood may dictate unusual realities if formed in abnormal circumstances. It is a time of structure-seeking, authority orientation, instant gratification, and general adaptation.

In the stage of CHILDHOOD, roughly from ages five or six to about twelve, the complex programming of his value system continues, powerfully impacted by role models or heroes. These may be sports heroes, show-business persons, or any one of a wide range of role models that impress the child. It is easy to understand how media, glitzing their "stars," can manufacture "personalities" controlled by advertisers not unaware of the economic benefits of their creations.

This stage represents the building and destruction of many a childhood dream. Sadly, for many their dream-machines become irreparably broken during this stage, and these youngsters grow to become adults who never seem able to imagine a better world. The childhood stage is characterized as a time of EXPLORATION, still retaining high needs for security and dependency, but also begins to accommodate spurting growth, limit-testing, the identification of individual skills and interests, and displays outwardly recognizable, distinctive, personality traits and behaviors.

During the ADOLESCENT years, a stage of personality development characterized by EXPERIMENTATION, the value-system is tested, modified and validated. The teenager, consumed by socialization processes relies heavily on mutual reinforcement by his peers. Authentic individuality is deeply cloaked by group and peer pressures. When asked why a person in this stage does a particular thing, they will respond, "Because everybody does it!" This is a stage of fads, outer-directedness, conflict, conformity, peer-orientation, willingness to challenge authority, formulation of skills and habits, and the search for identity.

Young John Mark seemed to betray his adolescent bearing when, after being taken by Paul and Barnabas on their missionary journey, he *"deserted them in Pamphylia, and had not continued with them in the work. They had such a sharp disagreement that they parted company. Barnabas took Mark and sailed for Cyprus, but Paul chose Silas and left."* (Acts 15:38ff)

Mark, raised with wealth and perhaps a little spoiled, had not yet fulfilled his promise by learning the value of commitment. Later, with maturity, he would learn his lessons, make the right choices, and perform admirably, writing the second gospel, among other accomplishments.

Somewhere around twenty years of age, many times coinciding with the college or early occupational years, the value-system and personality solidifies. Most people have successfully resolved the conflicts inherent at each stage of development and have moved on to the next plateau. Normally, it takes a significant emotional experience to change values once a person arrives here. Hence, the YOUNG ADULT, armed with a growing sense of self-awareness, assured of his growing skills, knowledge, and abilities, seeks the validation of his value-system and his essential self. It is a stage of APPLICATION. He is idealistic, visionary, open, normative, abstract, goal-oriented and aggressive. More than anything else, he "wants to do his thing." But from this stage, his assimilated values posture him for the rest of life.

Caleb wholly followed the Lord. The leader from the tribe of Judah developed flint-hard character which could not be eroded by the subsequent failings of his entire generation. When sent to spy out the promised land by Moses, he alone with Joshua, steadfastly resolved to go in and take the land. The quivering faithlessness of his peers, the resultant disillusionment and consequential forty years of desert wanderings did not at all dull his aspirations for conquering the land, but powerfully served to reinforce him in his quest. When the opportunity finally presented itself, Caleb was more than ready for the challenge and completed the task. J. Oswald Sanders would write,

> One most striking aspect of Caleb's triumph was that while not one of the young men of Israel—all his own contemporaries had died in the wilderness—succeeded in fully expelling the enemy from their territory, Caleb "drove thence the three sons of Anak."[3]

Cultural Programming

There exists another gigantic factor in the shaping of our value system, personality, and subsequent behavior. During the process of value formation, especially the last stages, significant world events have value-impacted large groups simultaneously. Shared experience programs individuals in similar ways. Some values undergo change, being substituted for new ones in response to new situations. Usually, it is the hierarchy which is rearranged, crucial values deemed less important, and lesser values taking on new meaning and application. While these events do not take on the status of a significant emotional experience, they do however create considerable responses within the personality.

Of these epochal events, let us examine briefly the great depression, World War II, the dawn of the post WWII nuclear age, technological change, and television and notice how these events have impacted our cultural and individual value shaping.

The Great Depression

The economic crash of 1929 and the great depression which followed profoundly affected the outlook of a generation that was raised during those years. It was a time of enormous trial; men unable to find work, their sense of worth shattered, shaken by economic need. Small wonder there arose a scale of values emphasizing thrift, conservation, self-reliance, responsibility, commitment, the family as the basic social and economic unit, and a host of other so-called "traditional values." Women were first housewife and mother. The male was the essential breadwinner, holding high regard for the employer who provided the job which enabled him and his family to exist.

World War II

World War II wrenched many young sons from their localities, dumped them together in groups heterogeneously, and shipped them to nearly all points of the earth. Patriotism was assumed and expected. Confronted with a plurality of cultures, their own growing value-systems bombarded with unheard of alternatives. Their traditional values would never look the same again. Women now began to make up a substantial portion of the workforce, beginning the slow, steady, and unrelenting dissolution of the family as the primary influence and shaper of values. The public schools began to assume that responsibility.

Nuclear War

The post-war malaise, brought on by the realities of living under the threat of megaton nuclear bombs, carried with it the sense of getting all the enjoyment possible for the moment. And there grew the unflinching hope of every American to fulfill the great American dream. If not for himself there was a strong notion to provide it for his children. During the 50's, upward social and economic mobility was passionately embraced. Mobility was now the norm. Even college students were expected to spend some of their summers traveling. Women continued in the marketplace, no longer as "Rosie the Riveter," but as a fixture in many sectors of commerce, if only in subordinate roles. Attitudes towards sexuality grew more liberal, the genteel romances of yesteryear beginning to give way to the more ribald manipulations of conquest for the male, and the capture mentality among women. Some observers labeled this period a time of "Take! Take!Take!" Educators, bolstered by a new intellectualism based on the theory of evolution and higher criticism of the Bible, began to substitute a secularism that was to permeate the entire public school system. Theologians debated the death of God. A high value of those maturing during these years became the unsatiated question of "Why?" and a growing acknowledgement of the restlessness and attending sense of meaningless that would permeate secular society.

Technological Change

Technological change has significantly impacted human values, and depending on what values one has adopted, not always for the best. Writing towards the end of the 60's, Emmanuel Mesthene, Director of Harvard's Program on Technology and Society, quotes Williams,

> "A society in which the store of knowledge concerning the consequences of action is large and rapidly increasing is a society in

> which received norms and their 'justifying' values will be increasingly subjected to questioning and reformulation."
>
> This is another way of pointing to the tension... between the need for social action based on knowledge on the one hand and the pull of traditional values on the other. The increased questioning and reformulation of values that Williams speaks of, coupled with a growing awareness that our values are in fact changing under the impact of technological change, leads many to believe that technology is by nature destructive to values. But this belief presupposes a conception of values as eternal and tends to confuse what is valuable with what is unchanging.[4]

It also points out the need to understand the difference between an "absolute" and a "relative" value system. Christians hold within their belief systems values which are unapologetically absolute: God, his redemptive purposes in history, the sanctity of the individual, work as calling, and so forth. Examples of relative values would be patriotism,, anti-war sentiment, family loyalty, parenting style, provincialism, mode of dress, political and economic ideologies such as capitalism, and so forth.

Television

If technological change generally must be considered bombastic, then television specifically must be understood as holocaustic in its impact on values. Generations have gleaned perceptions of reality wherein the most complex of human issues are handled in only one hour complete with four commercial breaks. Television has spawned a generation that is value-programmed to push buttons, constantly in search of amusement, and enraptured with competition to make the most startling and bizarre input in hope of breaking the incessant boredom of its watchers. Supreme instantism!

Generations ago, newspapers carried information in the form of tight little printed columns, a heyday for publishers, and these were read only by those who took the time to keep informed in an era when general literacy did not approach today's norms. During the last few decades, current events have flashed on TV screens in living rooms demanding that their beholders assimilate first hand their importance and meaning for them. And there have been some powerful messages for people being value-programmed during those events.

The chronicled assassination of JFK, certainly an American hero, taught a nation of idealists to comprehend tragedy. The deaths of Robert F. Kennedy, Martin Luther King, and others during the fermenting 60's embellished the thinking of those who experienced them as well as the themes of television journalism, reinforcing the growing suspicion of a nation not necessarily in control of its destiny.

Daily reports of Vietnam's carnage flooded the national psyche in living color, promoting deep and ultimate rationale for young people to disavow any sense of patriotism akin to that for which their forefathers willingly died. The sorrowful renouncement of continued office by Lyndon B. Johnson, his presidency victimized by the inability to win a war by sheer military and economic force, became for many another illustration of government's ineptitude and limited circumspection. The vestiges of idealistic dreams about a "great society" were already nightmares of the killing fields of Vietnam. Television grandly delivered these events to the living room.

The Watergate scandal's lengthy televised rehearsals, culminating in the Nixon resignation and subsequent pardon, carried with it the message, "Unlawful behaviors are OK, as long as you don't get caught."

Television has profoundly impacted attitudes about the nature of pair-bonding, marriage, the family, employer-employee relationships, money and credit, leisure time activities, the essential meaning of commitment and responsibility, and a host of other values through the years, the magnitude of its influence depending on when a person was value programmed.

However, some behavioral scientists identify certain building blocks of personality which are apparently common to all people, namely, heredity, environment, specific conditioning, and our choices. Let us examine these concepts a little more closely.

Heredity/Heritage

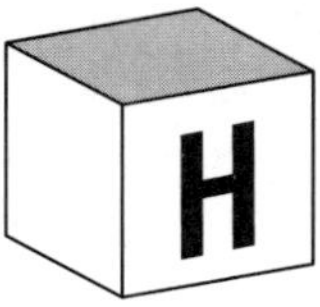

Jesus asked a rhetorical question in the sermon on the mount, *"But which of you by taking thought is able to add to his stature one cubit?"* (Matt. 6:27)

The ancient measure of a cubit was approximately 18 inches. While most any contemporary basketballer would opt for that much additional height, it still isn't available merely for the taking. We come with a certain physical package: the color of our eyes, the shade of our skin, our somatotype, that is, our physique, our level of intelligence, our position in the birth order in the family, and so forth. While it is possible to slightly modify some of these facets of personality, traits, and gifts, they are for the most part "givens," i.e., we are not able to change them to any significant degree.

With wisdom comes the realization that you cannot change history. What has been done is done. So it remains with events that occurred before we were born ... our heritage. We had nothing to do with the way things unfolded before we were here. We did not chose the family, town, country, political, and economic systems into which we were born. This is another set of "givens" affecting us profoundly.

There is a sense in which a church denominational heritage has provided a range of possible environments and subsequent choices which tend to shape us before we are even aware of their influences upon us. For example, certain denominational mores have been handed down through generations that strongly exert pressures on behavior. A person brought up within a strong fundamentalist orientation may hold attitudes about the role of education which for him may be largely unexamined. If raised in the south, he may have no qualms about smoking, but alcoholic beverages are a taboo. He might rely on these attitudes just as surely as his genetic gifts. His cousin, raised in another denomination, will condemn the smoker as an abuser of the body as the holy temple of God's residing Spirit in the believer, and drink wine at communion.

Environment

There may always exist urgent debate about the fine line between heredity and environment. Both factors play distinctive parts in human development and behavior. The concept of "organismic readiness" illustrates how these two basic factors work.

A parent may attempt to "potty-train" an infant, trying all sorts of reward stimulations, and mental games with the infant, but until the child is old enough to comprehend and process the message, physically developed to the point of being able to exercise control over bowel movements, there will be no success by the parent regarding potty-training. The organism, operating with complete system functionality, will behave and perform only when it is able to perform. Certain genetically patterned developmental processes become ready to operate at appropriate stages and perform their normal tasks when the environment makes demands on the systems, but only after they have developed their capabilities.

Paul instructed Timothy not to appoint a person who was a recent convert to the office of "overseer" or bishop, because "he may become conceited and fall under the same judgment as the devil." (I Tim.3:6) Lacking the discernment that comes with spiritual development, he could not possibly be expected to behave appropriately.

The Birth Order Book depicts another interaction between heredity and environment in its portrayal of certain types of behavior that are shaped by the position in the family into which a person is born. There seems to be a body of evidence pointing to the development of certain consistent behaviors of the oldest, second oldest, middle child, and youngest sibling. There are forces shaping behavior as the genetic blossoming of personality unfolds.

Specific Conditioning

Missionary Thom Hopler, writing in *A World of Difference*[5], entitled the first chapter, “How much did you pay for your wife?” “The question tumbled from the lips of an old man during the first month Marcia and I spent in Kenya. When I explained that we don’t sell women in America, he laughed and said, squeezing Marcia’s thin arm, ‘I wouldn’t give a goat for her either.’”

The book, subtitled “Following Christ Beyond Your Cultural Walls,” issued from Thom’s life of service. Spending ten years of his life communicating Christ under the auspices of the African Inland Mission, he overcame significant cultural barriers of his own as he prepared for a ministry in missions. Thom made a choice to attend a Bible college, selecting an environment where specific experiences would reinforce the profound inner calling that he sensed by his eighteenth birthday. Growing up in the megalopolis of northern New Jersey, he did not always appreciate racial differences. The Lord apprehended Thom in a very special way, changing a somewhat rebellious motorcycle-driving teenager complete with the normative black leather jacket into a supremely loving, sensitive, and caring person whose mind was uniquely quickened by God. He would one day recount a portentous incident from the early 1960s:

> There was a movement in Africa to remove anything associated with colonialism, including Christianity. The parliament of Kenya debated this issue quite seriously. At one point a non-Christian in the parliament said, in essence, “We are a tribalistic people. We each have our own gods, our own ideals, our own understanding of right and wrong. But these are not adequate to meet the needs of our own nation. With Christianity

has come a system of values that supercedes tribalism. We hold our young people accountable on the basis of the Bible. If we take away the Bible, whose tribal system will we adopt in its place?"

The parliament agreed. The people had stopped killing each other because the Bible said, "Thou shalt not kill." As they discussed it further, they decided to make it mandatory to teach the Bible in all the schools of Kenya. Other religions have come into competition with Christianity, but they still require that some more universal system of values be taught. They recognize that without values, people become dangerous. God does not desire to destroy our values but to lift them to a higher plane.[6]

The opposite is happening in the west. As we secularize and move away from biblical values, we are finding it more and more difficult to maintain order, to maintain even a low level of sociability. Thus we should not encourage other cultures simply to dump their values, which allow for a degree of peace. Rather we should show a better way.[7]

Choices

The most dynamic building block of personality is the ability to make choices. The very offer of biblical salvation is dependent on the ability to make the choice of receiving Christ as Lord. With our ability to choose we may become kings or bums, scholars or simpletons, rich or poor, bond or free. But increasingly, we hone our skills in decision-making by the constant exercise of our daily choices.

There is the story about a brazen youngster who was tired of constantly being reproved by the headmaster at his school because of his poor choices and resulting behavior. He decided to try to show up the learned teacher, and so captured a small bird, and holding it in his hand, approached the educator and asked, "Tell me, sir, is this creature in my hand dead or alive?" He knew that he would prove the man wrong whatever way he responded. If he said it was dead, he could open his hand and let it fly away. If he said it was alive, a tight squeeze would also show him up to be incorrect. "Well, what is it, teacher?"

The headmaster turned and simply said, "Son, it's your choice!"

When it comes to deciding who you shall become, how to respond to the forces that would shape you, it is always "your choice!"

Nowhere is this more apparent than in choosing the kind of leader that you can become. The force of the following chapters lies in the opportunity for every authentic believer to choose to love, and then to implement that agape love through the manner in which they choose to influence others. The leadership of love demands a continuous decision to love as Jesus loves.

A function-flow diagram suggests:

It appears that many factors shape personality, and from each distinct personality style emerges a natural leadership style. But to become a loving leader, we must make a choice and carry it forward with resolve.

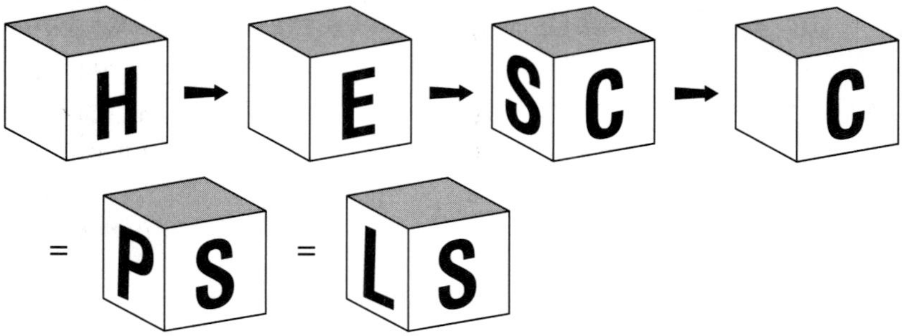

Notes

1. Wrightsman, Lawrence S., and Fillmore H. Sandford. *Psychology: A Scientific Study of Human Behavior.* Monterey, CA: Brooks/Cole Publishing Co., 1975, p 411.

2. Morris Massy, videotape series entitled, "What You Are Is Where You Were When." Farmington, MI: Magnetic Video Corporation, 1976
3. Sanders, J. Oswald. *Spiritual Manpower*. Chicago: Moody Press, 1965, p. 88.
4. Mesthene, Emmanuel. *Technological Change*. New York: New American Library, 1970.
5. Hopler, Thom. *A World of Difference: Following Christ Beyond Your Cultural Walls*. Downers Grove, IL: InterVarsity Christian Fellowship of the United States of America, 1981.
6. Ibid.
7. Ibid.

WIMPIER AND WEAKER

We decided to visit family in Mesa, Arizona, over Thanksgiving. Our own daughter was now grown and married, but we still took time to help other children. Now we had Israel, a stocky, robust, ten-year-old, himself a product of a former foster child. We were all returning to grandma's house with our two nephews after monitoring the boy's swim in the neighborhood pool when Israel served notice of his desired territorial rights concerning the lone bicycle among three boys.

"I get the bike first because I'm bigger and stronger!"

James, a slender and cautious one responded, "I think I should get it first. I'm wimpier and weaker."

CALVIN AND HOBBES By Bill Watterson

Dictatorata

GO ARROGANTLY AMID PEACE AND TRANQUILITY, AND REMEMBER WHAT GREAT SATISFACTION THERE CAN BE IN GRABBING CONTROL, AS FAR AS POSSIBLE WITHOUT APOLOGY BULLY INTO OTHER PEOPLE'S SPACE. Boast your views loudly and often; the more you are seen and recognized the more believable you are perceived. ❧ ❧ ❧ Appear to listen to others, even the slow and incompetent; they can be manipulated. Surround yourself with the weak and incognizant. While they are of little value, you will look good by comparison. ❧ ❧ Advance yourself. Always take credit for any achievements whether they are yours or not. Make sure that your agenda supercedes everything and everyone. Look out for number one. ❧ ❧ Be selfish in all business and personal affairs; master the art of half-truths and doublespeak. What others do not know cannot hurt you. Never use candor. Especially do not feign weakness; your power lies in projections of status. ❧ ❧ Take kindly the counsel of years, gracefully clinging to your rights and each vestige of authority. Nurture a deep-seated suspicion for those who trust. You never have, why should they? Therefore, when things go wrong, find an appropriate scapegoat. Build on current prejudices. You are the master of your fate, you make things happen. Your paradigms and priorities have always been correct. The universe exists for your benefit. ❧ ❧ ❧ With all of the world's problems, conflicts and needs, take delight in the realization that you got yours first. Forget about others. Strive to be ostentatious.

Found in a contemporary book about leadership, 1990.

Leadership Consultants International
Vista, California
619-941-1000

CHAPTER FOUR

Seeking Power Without God: The Authoritarian Syndrome

But Jesus said, "You know that the rulers of the Gentiles lord it over them, and their great men exercise authority over them. It shall not be so among you; but whoever would be great among you must be your servant, and whoever would be first among you must be your slave; even as the Son of man came not to be served but to serve, and to give his life as a ransom for many." (Matt. 20:25ff)

We have seen how the development of personality is influenced by many factors, but it must be clearly understood that the involvement of God in personality development has the most exciting and profound impact. As an illustration, it may be wise to investigate how the formulation of personality without God's touch occurs. The Bible speaks of a natural man, uninfluenced by the revelations of God, unregenerated by the Holy Spirit, and attempting to find meaning and purpose in life. He makes certain inevitable choices. Sadly, there are elements of this personality which have invaded a significant number of leaders in contemporary Christendom. There is spiritual immaturity that glares from many pulpits and boardrooms alike as many are unwilling to capitulate fully to the claims of Christ and take the necessary steps to spiritual growth and freedom. The consequences bode ill for these leaders and the organizations which they direct.

One concept may stand as a sweeping generalization, but not without merit when examined in the light of these considerations. It is the notion of "*insecurity*," which suggests many kinds of things. I believe an ultimate biblical understanding of the person who is basically insecure will reveal a person who has not discovered and applied the love of God to his life. All of the resounding and supportive promises of God's word are null and void to such a person. He is left only to his own devices as a means of gaining value, purpose, direction and meaning in life. Faced with a competitive world, many individuals develop feelings of inadequacy when they compare themselves to others who seemingly have their lives together, and appear successful. Time will not be given here to examine all the reasons people feel insecure, but the following discussion describes one type or syndrome of personality development that occurs with constant repetition in human behavior and illustrates certain levels of insecurity.

Shortly after World War II, an imposing volume labeled *The Authoritarian Personality* [1] was published. It captured the attention of many scholars for its research and portrayal of a coherent "*syndrome of personality*." It made psychological sense of diverse forms of social irrationality. Although the authors avowed interest was anti-semitic prejudice and post-war pro-fascist attitudes, their findings seemed to cast light on other considerations:

> ...on modes of leadership and followership, on styles and consequences of teaching and learning, on true believers of various stripes, and particularly on what Hofstader has since called the paranoid trend in political life. Here was a major

> attempt to trace in psychological terms the linkage between personality and ideology.[1]

The authors provided a solid concept, a wealth of evidence and even a measuring instrument they named "the F scale," to determine the objective measure of authoritarianism. M. Brewster Smith in his foreword for *Dimensions of Authoritarianism*, defines the concept thus:

> Authoritarianism characterizes the basically weak and dependent person who has sacrificed his capacity for genuine experience of self and others so as to maintain a precarious sense of order and safety that is psychologically necessary for him. In the type case, the authoritarian confronts with a facade of spurious strength a world in which rigidly stereotyped categories are substituted for the affectionate and individualized experience of which it is incapable. Such a person is estranged from inner values and lacks self-awareness. His judgments are governed by a punitive conventional moralism, reflecting external standards towards which he remains insecure since he has failed to make them really his own. His relations with others depend on considerations of power, success, and adjustment, in which people figure as means rather than as ends, and achievement is valued competitively rather than for its own sake. In his world, the good, the powerful, and the ingroup merge to stand in fundamental opposition to the immoral, the weak, the outgroup. For all that he seeks to align himself with the former, his underlying feelings of weakness and self-contempt commit him to a constant and embittered struggle to prove to himself and others that he really belongs to the strong and good, and that his ego-alien impulses, which he represses, belong to the weak and bad.[2]

Such a definition, though born of psychoanalytic research, presents a picture of a personality type that has been common throughout the ages of mankind. If the definition holds true, then it should be possible to journey through history and literature and find significant pictures of this personality syndrome. Is this not an array of behaviors and attitudes that seems pervasive in contemporary society? Let us examine and review some pertinent concepts from the behavioral sciences and other writings to see if in fact this kind of person has been among us, perhaps since man has used language and experienced social interaction.

WEAK AND DEPENDENT

The first characteristic of this person is that he exhibits a personality both weak and dependent. What happens in human development to make a person weak and dependent?

Erik Erikson, a noted psychoanalytic spokesman, provided a theory of personality development which is commonly called "The Eight Stages of Man." Erikson showed that people develop through stages in which they deal with certain developmental tasks with an either/or determination. That is, they go through phases of development in which they either cope successfully, or they move on to the next stage without being ready for its new challenges. Whether the outcome is governed by subconscious effort or direct decisions, choices are made in order for the individual to move on in another step toward maturity.

Dealing with these alternatives is an overwhelmingly important occurrence in human development, for it involves the element of trust, how comfortable we are with our circumstances. Indeed, Erikson stated that the first phase of life entails acquiring a sense of basic trust while overcoming a basic sense of mistrust:

> He develops a sense of expectancy through a mixture of trust and mistrust. His sense of basic trust—as opposed to a sense of basic mistrust—becomes the critical theme in his first development phase. For the neonate, a sense of trust requires a feeling of physical comfort and a minimum experience of fear or uncertainty. If these are assured him, he will extend his trust to new experiences. In contrast, a sense of mistrust arises from unsatisfactory physical and psychological experiences and leads to fearful apprehension of future situations.

> A sense of basic trust helps the individual to grow psychologically and to accept new experiences willingly. Each successful outcome of his trust tends to produce favorable expectations of new experiences, which will, however, always offer occasion of mistrust.[3]

For Erikson, then, the picture is not extremely complicated. There are stages one goes through, either successfully resolving and learning that which is necessary for continued future development, or a negativistic, incipient pathology occurs. His eight stages of man reflect this principle:

Phase I: Acquiring a Sense of Basic Trust While Overcoming a Sense of Basic Mistrust—A Realization of Hope.
Phase II: Acquiring a Sense of Autonomy While Combating a Sense of Doubt and Shame—A Realization of Will.
Phase III: Acquiring a Sense of Initiative and Overcoming a Sense of Guilt—A Realization of Purpose.
Phase IV: Acquiring a Sense of Industry and Fending Off a Sense of Inferiority—A Realization of Competence.
Phase V: Acquiring A Sense of Identity While Overcoming a Sense of Identity Diffusion—A Realization of Fidelity.
Phase VI: Acquiring a Sense of Intimacy and Solidarity and Avoiding a Sense of Isolation—A Realization of Love.
Phase VII: Acquiring a Sense of Generativity and Avoiding a Sense of Self-Absorption—A Realization of Care.
Phase VIII:Acquiring a Sense of Integrity and Avoiding a Sense of Despair—A Realization of Wisdom.

It appears, then, that the person who later becomes the typical authoritarian personality is one who has not learned a basic sense of trust and, as a result, harbors attitudes of self-condemnation, guilt, and shame. Compared to the person who finds his sufficiency in a relationship with God based on forgiveness and grace, this is an extremely significant developmental coping posture.

INCAPACITY TO EXPERIENCE SELF AND OTHERS

The second facet of the Authoritarian personality syndrome is the incapacity for a "genuine experience of self and others." Earl Jabay, in his book *The God Players*,[4] indicated some basic patterns of mis-evaluation that are all too common in people who refuse to utilize appropriate patterns of evaluation and feedback which produce satisfactory responses and lifestyles.

> Perhaps the most basic choice a person makes is the way he chooses to see himself. Almost invariably, we see ourselves as though through the wrong end of a telescope. Our introspective eyes, seeing only what we want to see, create a self-portrait in which we appear to be immature, small, innocent, victimized, too hindered by overwhelming circumstances to act much differently and too lacking in an awareness of our freedom to bear responsibility. That is, our self-image is always a flattering miniature of what we are in reality. You notice that I hedge a little on these generalizations.[5]

The authoritarian is one who has forsaken an instantaneous, congruent (i.e., an effectively coordinated way of thinking, feeling, and language), and spontaneous orientation because he has set a standard for himself that is unrealistic and he will not bring himself into phase with these expectations. The willingness to choose a grandiose or at the same time miniature view of himself is typical of man, again according to the perspective of Jabay:

> ...we characteristically see ourselves in miniature. Such a view might be called the natural view of man. We come by it naively. Once gotten, it is comfortable and easy to keep throughout life. If space would permit, we could trace how this miniature view of man is given wide application in modern, behavioral science, and no less in the various branches of Christian theology. The image of man as a struggling, basically righteous, evolving, learning and laudable individual is very precious to the human heart.

There is a close relationship between the miniature and grandiose view we have of ourselves. These views are opposite sides of the same coin. That is, where we find one in a person, we also find the other—and usually to the same degree of distortedness. Our distortedness, of course, may be subconscious, but it does not prevent us from having a decided preference for the miniature view as the basis of our life. The miniature view, (a) gives us a feeling of being right, (b) merely encourages us to grow a little more and (c) keeps us from making any difficult changes. The grandiose, godlike view of ourselves, on the other hand, is quite intolerable when we are conscious of it because (a) we feel guilty about it, (b) we sense that our godishness should go, and (c) that painful changes are in order."[6]

RIGIDITY TO MAINTAIN ORDER AND SAFETY

The third major facet of the type A person, as the Authoritarian personality has familiarly been called, is a necessary rigidity to maintain a precarious sense of order and safety. This aspect of the syndrome can be understood on the basis of the fairly common patterns of misevaluation that are more easily recognizable from the perspective of the general semanticist:

> The general semanticist is not so much interested in the grammatical structure of the language as he is in its implicatory structure. If we make a statement about persons, things, or events, what does it imply that we will find out about their structure if we go out and look at them? Note that he does not ask what a thing is, but rather how is it being used: not what is he, but what does he say? If we say that he is a Communist, the language implies a simplicity not to be found when we go look at him. It implies that we have a nice, neat, sharp definition of Communist which will fit all to whom the label is applied. It implies that he will act the way we say that Communists act in all situations and at all times, and it implies that our definition of Communist is the only possible valid one. There are apparently many people who use this simple verbal map which fits no known territory when we try to check it. The structure of the language is not

> similar to the structure of the situation.
>
> When our maps do not fit the territory, when we act as if our inferences are factual knowledge, we prepare ourselves for a world that is not there. If this happens often enough, the inevitable result is frustration and an ever-increasing tendency to warp the territory to fit our maps. We see what we want to see, and the more we see it, the more likely we are to reinforce the distorted perception in the familiar circular and spiral feedback pattern.[7]

The general semanticist's world view reflected in Alfred Korzybski's *Science and Sanity*[8] circumscribes this measure of the syndrome when he speaks of patterns of miscommunication and, more specifically, the "intensional" orientation. Such a person is overly absorbed with the maps of language and loses sight of the territory of life and the event levels of experience. He has lost his ability to respond "phenomenologically," that is, the ability to perceive each situation, person, and experience as a one-of-kind occurrence. He guides himself by words alone, being somewhat oblivious of context. He is conscious of similarities, but not keen on differences, prone to explaining words by definitions only. Characterized by a disregard of observation, he acts as though words were things, predisposing himself to automatic reactions to symbols, as compared to life to life encounters with others.

This ingrown, intensional, semantic pattern parallels the prejudices of the authoritarian character. His stereotyped and rigid orientation which breeds prejudice may possibly stem from an unwillingness to expend the necessary energy for developing alternative ways of perceiving situations, persons or objects. This type of coping is attributable to the unloving, uninterested posture of one who is supremely preoccupied with matters of self concern.

When an individual's behavior makes himself the object of an accusing conscience and is unwilling to make the concessions to change necessary to assuage that conscience, he siphons off energies towards selfish concerns. De Bono's reflections become almost humorous when considered in this light when he states:

> It is disturbing to think how many situations are incompletely understood because attempts at explanation persist in using well-tried familiar patterns which ought themselves to be re-examined.[9]

So fundamentally, the authoritarian person has, in order to maintain his sense of orderliness without threat-level concerns, developed patterns of mis-evaluation. In so doing he has forfeited his ability to be genuine and has short-circuited basic means of feedback which could correct his path.[10]

CONSIDERATIONS FOR POWER

Simply stated then, if a person is unfulfilled, understanding that changes are in order, but either lacking the rationale for the change or the willingness to make such changes, then utilizes patterns of misevaluation, he apparently needs only to seek power to accomplish the syndrome of authoritarianism.

Viktor Frankl, emerging from the German concentration camp at Auschwitz, wrote in his autobiography *Man's Search for Meaning*, "Only if one's original concern with meaning fulfillment is frustrated is one ... content with power."[11]

Such a desire for power is not an unusual response to feelings of personal inadequacy. It would be typical of the Freudian defense mechanism of overcompensation. For one who is unwilling to make necessary changes in behavior, other excuses and avenues represent bonafide circumvention to the threatening experiences. That such self-manipulation is inherently detrimental in the long run can be illustrated by the parallel and antiquitous concept of HUBRIS which grew out of the Golden Age of Greece. Here we see the concept of power coupled with the familiar pattern of misevaluation instilled by pathologically oriented pride. W.G. deBurgh writes of HUBRIS:

> Its root meaning is the violent overstepping of the mark, the insolence of triumph, and the pride of life that tramples underfoot the unwritten laws of gods and man. "Hubris" is the closest Greek equivalent for "sin." Its most characteristic application was to the insatiable thirst for power which drives

> a man or a nation headlong as though possessed by a demon, on the path of unbridled self-assertion. This blinding passion, outraging alike personal liberty and public law, lures the victim in a frenzy of self-confidence towards destruction. It provokes nemesis, the feeling of righteous indignation, in the gods and in his fellow men.[12]

Barclay cites two other significant thoughts accentuating HUBRIS. One was the strange concept of the "envy of the gods," which asserts that the gods begrudged man all happiness, prosperity and success; and it goes back as far as Homer. The other was the resulting terror of success because success was bound to awaken the envy of the gods:

> Seek not to become Zeus. Mortal things befit a mortal. If anyone shall possess wealth and shall excel others in beauty, and have won distinction by display of strength in the games, let him not forget that his raiment is on mortal limbs, and that the earth shall be his garment at the last.[13]

But to the Greeks, HUBRIS went far beyond the terribly contemptuous insolence to produce the sheer desire to deliberately hurt other people for the purpose of humiliation. Aristotle describes it fully:

> Insolence (hubris) is another form of slight, as being an act of injury or annoyance involving the disgrace of the sufferer, not for the sake of any benefit to the agent beyond the mere fact of its having been done, but only for his personal gratification; for the requital of injuries is not insolence (hubris), but revenge. The source of the pleasure found in insolent action in the feeling that in injuring others we are claiming an exceptional superiority to them. [Rhetoric 2][14]

These insights concerning an antiquitous concept give fodder to the realization that while the language used to discern the various concepts has evolved, the events themselves have been understood, at times deeply, by brilliant minds.

Erich Fromm, in his book *Escape From Freedom*, considers the same territory but from the viewpoint of man's unbearable loneliness.

He speaks of a "tendency to give up one's own individual self and fuse one's self with somebody or something outside of one's self in order to acquire the strength which the individual self is lacking." After discussing the masochistic trends which are so similar to the Jabayan views of self-deprecation with a purpose, Fromm explains the sadistic tendencies, typical of the Grecian HUBRIS, in its affinity to strike out at other people. His handling of the unconscious rationalization that occurs in the authoritarian mind is exhibited:

> Sadistic tendencies for obvious reasons are usually less conscious and more rationalized than the socially more harmless masochistic trends. Often they are covered up by reaction formations of overgoodness or overconcern for others. Some of the most frequent rationalizations are the following: 'I rule over you because I know what is best for you, and in your own interest you should follow me without opposition.' Or, 'I am so wonderful and unique that I have a right to expect that other people become dependent on me.' Another rationalization that often covers the exploiting tendencies is, 'I have done so much for you, and now I am entitled to take from you what I want.' The more aggressive kind of sadistic impulse finds its most frequent rationalization in two forms: 'I have been hurt by others and my wish to hurt them is nothing but retaliation,' or, 'By striking first I am defending myself or my friends against the danger of being hurt.'[15]

Finally, it seems intriguing and beyond the incidences of happenstance that the brilliant mind of Shakespeare has presented us with an almost too good type case in Iago from Othello. Could such a case bubble from the pen of even so great a mind if the observations of the syndrome were not so readily available?

Iago is one of Shakespeare's most subtle villains. He is an Italian and, therefore, in Elizabethan eyes malignant by nature. Iago loves mischief for its own sake and finds cruelty amusing. He believes all woman are false, and if Desdemona is true to Othello it is because so far she has had no chance to be otherwise. Yet even so, given this character, why did he act as he did? Coleridge spoke of Iago's "motiveless malignity." Hazlitt replied that Iago's motive was a perverted love of power:

> Iago is a professional soldier. He has climbed up from the lowest rank until he is now within reach of the top. He naturally expects that Othello will select him as second in command, and his vanity is in part justified, for he is in many ways a greater man than Cassio. When he is rejected, he suffers the bitter blow that will come to everyone at some time or other when he sees himself passed over in favor of someone whom he despises. Injured vanity is a wrong to the essential self. This is the main cause of Iago's anger. It is not a dignified cause. Hence he refuses to face it out with his own conscience. He shies away from the sour truth that Othello considers Cassio to be a better soldier than himself. He begins to invent causes for Othello's choice—any excuse to get even with Othello. At any cost he will ease the writhing anguish of his hurt vanity by destroying those who have wronged him and all that they value most. These things are revealed in his soliloquies. Iago therefore begins with a lust to hurt both Othello and Cassio through Desdemona, but he soon becomes fascinated by his own cleverness and inextricably and fatally entangled in his own plot. Not the least of Iago's subtlety is that he seems always to be keeping something back, to know more than he reveals.[16]

The syndrome of authoritarianism apparently generates from developmental alternatives. If certain needs are met, then other stages follow. If they are not met, then different alternatives and behaviors ensue. In other words, the "type A" personality is learned; moreover, it is a coping response that develops out of a given set of conditions.

INCIPIENCE

The authoritarian person, existing in a twilight zone between reality and non-reality, displays strengths by his ability to simplify, promote, and manipulate ideas which, although not ultimately satisfying because of their incongruity, nevertheless provide an alluring shortcut for other dependent persons who may ever be on the alert for the easy way. This attractiveness, of course, affords the opportunity for the manipulation of others for his own benefit and power. It can be illustrated in a number of ways:

1. It takes a strong person to assume leadership in emergency or crisis situations. The very strength and ability to conceptualize situations in a manner that calls for his own dominant emergence, frequently spawns the seeds for the change of benevolent autocrats to the dibilatatious authoritarian leader. In times of crisis or uncertainty, directives must be clear and concise, or followers will be unable to mobilize for appropriate activity. But over the long haul of organizational or group growth, the same rhetoric becomes cliche' and simply an instrument for retaining status, power, and control. The emerging leader must be able to grow along with his group, or he inevitably deflects towards the authoritarian syndrome.

2. Rank has its privileges, so frequently displayed by bureaucratic experiences, and it is not difficult for the leader to become more enchanted with maintaining his own role and power. When this unfortunate incidence occurs, such as a pastor falling in love with his pastoral office more than for his love for the Lord, sooner or later he fails to develop others, or accomplish other tasks, and he becomes the the ultimate organizational cork, bottlenecking spontaneity, creativity, and fosters authoritarianism. Sadly, many followers unconsciously begin to emulate this role model, and the non-caring, power-brokers' attitude begins to permeate the organization. When such a person is also firmly established in organizational gate-keeping roles, the authoritarian syndrome may become magnified; the delights of power easily leading to a fixation in this role.

3. Another common seed for authoritarianism in the leadership process occurs when the importance of the group's tasks overshadows or eliminates the dignity and worth of the individual and his needs. The "ends justifying the means" mentality can promote manipulation far easier than honest confrontation and collaboration of all involved.

Highly competitive situations breed this sort of task fulfilling priority structure where those in positions of power limit alternative means of influence, even and especially in the form of ideas. The rationale most commonly cited is, "we don't have time" for inclusion of those without sufficient levels of status.

4. Lastly, what Robert K. Merton called "value homophily," the phenomenon of the tendency of people of like opinions and values to seek each other out as companions, can be another force leading to the development of authoritarian behaviors in groups and individuals. It is found in the benefits of conformity:

> To the extent that a group is attractive for an individual, and to the extent that he desires acceptance as a member of that group, he will be motivated—whether he is aware of it or not—to accept the group's outlook.[17]

This demand for conformity by dependent individuals often produces the seduction of leaders to fixate in their leadership stance ... again, a seed of authoritarianism.

When the Lord is left out of life's equation, it is easy to understand how individuals substitute their own sense of importance, careening to concerns for power, status and control in attempts to find the meaning and purpose which sadly eludes them. When Paul wrote to the church at Rome, he put the situation succinctly when he described the natural man: *"They exchanged the truth of God for a lie, and worshiped and served created things rather than the Creator ...."* To get all wrapped up in one's self is a pretty small world.

Notes

1. Adorno, T.W., and others. *The Authoritarian Personality.* New York: W.W. Norton & Company, Inc., 1950.
2. Kirscht, John P., and Ronald C. Dillehay. *Dimensions of Authoritarianism: A Review of Research and Theory.* Lexington, KY: University of Kentucky Press, 1967.
3. Maier, Henry W. *Three Theories of Child Development.* New York: Harper and Row, 1969.

4. Jabay, Earl. *The God Players*. Grand Rapids: Zondervan, 1969.
5. Ibid.
6. Ibid.
7. Weinberg, Harry L. *Levels of Knowing and Existence*. New York: Harper and Row, 1969.
8. Korzybski, Alfred. *Science and Sanity*. Lancaster, PA: Science Press, 1933.
9. De Bono, Edward. *New Think*. New York: Avon Publishers, 1968.
10. Rokeach, Milton. *The Open and Closed Mind*. New York: Basic Books, 1960.
11. Frankl, Victor E. *Man's Search for Meaning: An Introduction to Logotherapy*. New York: Pocket Books, 1959.
12. Barclay, William. *More New Testament Words*. New York: Harper and Brothers, 1958.
13. Ibid.
14. Ibid.
15. Fromm, Erich. *Escape From Freedom*. New York: Avon Publishers, 1965.
16. Harrison, G.B., ed. *Shakespeare: Major Plays and Sonnets*. New York: Harcourt, Brace, 1948.
17. Katz, Elihu, and Paul F. Lazarfeld. *Personal Influence*. New York: The Free Press of Glenco, 1964.

MASTER OF THE SECOND-GUESS

I fidgeted on my seat that fateful September night when, with only three games remaining in the '89 season, the Padres lost their last chance to tie the pennant. It was a most incredible game. The Padres needed to win once more against Cincinnati right here, right now, to force the next weeks' season ending series with the division-leading Giants into a showdown. The odds were against them, but there was still hope. The Giants suddenly appeared vulnerable, losing to the Dodgers. Now, with the Padres behind in a brilliantly pitched game 1-0, they had rallied in the bottom of the ninth to tie the game 1-1. During the next three innings I still see in my mind's eye about seven different hard shots from Padre bats that backed outfielders to the wall only to fall inches short of the gamewinner. The tension was thrilling, electric, exacerbating!

Then in the thirteenth inning THE DECISION was made. That choice to pitch to Eric Davis! I couldn't believe it. First base was open. Davis has to be the best that the Reds have to offer. I agreed with the chant of a fan behind me who yelled to the fifth Padre pitcher, Calvin Shiraldi, "Do not, I repeat, DO NOT throw this man a strike!" Of course Shiraldi did, and Davis clubbed a double off the left field wall, driving in what would be the winning run. My silence echoed throughout the stadium. The immense crowd sensed that this was a mortal blow that the Pads couldn't overcome, and they didn't.

As I walked to the car, I wondered how manager Jack Mc Keon could have made the decision to pitch to Davis. I had worked with Mc Keon when I was a consultant to the Padres organization, creating and implementing a personal developmental program for the players, and performing other organizational developmental tasks. Mc Keon was astute. He had hung in there when times were tough, and he continued to take the long view, no shortcuts for expediency. He stood as a leader with values and integrity. He was a supreme judge of talent and a knowledgeable baseball man. He evidenced rare curiosity and was a leader-learner. Jack was simply a rare person—a genuine winner. I felt for Jack, but there was something incongruous about the happening I had just witnessed that just wouldn't figure. I couldn't verbalize it. I just sensed something was wrong with the conclusion that baldly continued to crash in my mind. Dumbest play that I could imagine!

The next day I experienced a paradigm shift!

The morning paper told the story of how Jack and his cast of coaches sought from Shiraldi who HE would rather pitch to. It was the kind of input that a secure and aware manager should elicit. It was the kind of information that would be requested from a manager who recognized that it was the pitcher, the player, who would win or lose the ballgame....no matter what was decided. It was a question from a secure person who knew that whatever strategy was to be implemented would have to be "owned" by the players who were to implement it. Sure the pennant was on the line. What better place to reinforce the fact that the pitcher has worth and dignity, that he comes with a mind and the ability to make pertinent choices also … .those choices that he will have to carry out!

Then it all made sense to me, and my admiration for Jack returned, reinforced to higher levels. Here was a guy who could and did make the best choices in the toughest, most testing of circumstances. He showed once again that he was the MANAGER, not the ball player. And he demonstrated wisdom. Who knows whether or not the next guy would have hit Shiraldi just as hard … and it really doesn't matter. One at-bat does not a season make. There are one hundred sixty two games. What was important was that the pitcher knew that he was the man of the hour, and that the entire organization was behind him … at the critical moment. I would venture that anyone on the pitching staff again realized that the game is theirs to win or lose ... with the support of management to do their best, secure in their own level of confidence. Baseball is always a game of "next times" for those who come out second best. My guess is that next time, Shiraldi will make his best decision, and throw his best pitch. What more is there?

CHAPTER FIVE

Paradigms ... Shifting and Otherwise

According to the American Heritage Dictionary: PAR.A.DIGM. n. any example or model, from Greek paradeigma, model, from paradeiknumai, to compare, to exhibit: para = alongside + deiknumai, to show.

Paradigms have been defined as the way we look at life, in essence our world-view. But they are representations of realities, depictions of things which are held up alongside the phenomenon under examination and compared to it in order to determine if it is an accurate portrayal of that which we want to scrutinize. Growing up during WWII I remember that it was common for youngsters to make models of airplanes and battleships which were being used in the war. They were minutely detailed replicas of the real tools of battle. But paradigms also represent models of ideas, how we think about things, critically and otherwise.

Some of these are models we painlessly assimilate through our heritage and upbringing, cultural environment, language and learning. They become our filters of reality, our understanding of the way things are, how humans behave, the manner in which groups and systems operate, and even our finite understanding of an infinite God. They are quite important to us as we make our separate journeys through life, supremely affecting not only our ideas about the world in which we live, but also shaping our perceptions of our very own selves.

The creation-evolution debate probably illustrates this point as well as any. It logically follows that a person will look differently on another person depending on whether that other person is a biological mistake, an evolutionary happenstance, or a uniquely ordered creation, one of a certain level of being bearing the imprimatur of the Artist in his person.

Paradigms are similar to values in that some are better than others. But paradigms are either more right or wrong, more correct or incorrect. They are remarkable like maps. They either work and are functional, or they are misleading and provide misleading information when implemented.

Take for instance the Freudian model that depicts human behavior as a bell-shaped curve with normal people in the middle, the neurotic individuals on one side and psychotic persons on the other side. The paradigm suggests that when there exists an overabundance of stress, for example, a person may cross over certain thresholds and become abnormal, deflecting in either of the two directions, thereby implying that at any time one can experience temporary insanity. This model has been swallowed by the legal system of the United States and even used successfully as a defense in the near assassination of former president Reagan.

A better paradigm was suggested by O. Hobart Mowrer, former

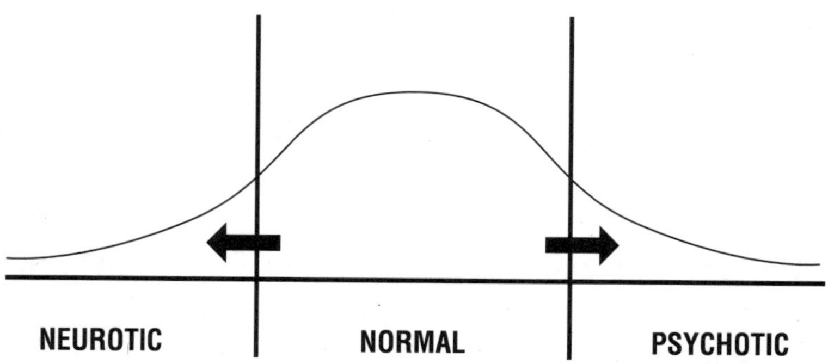

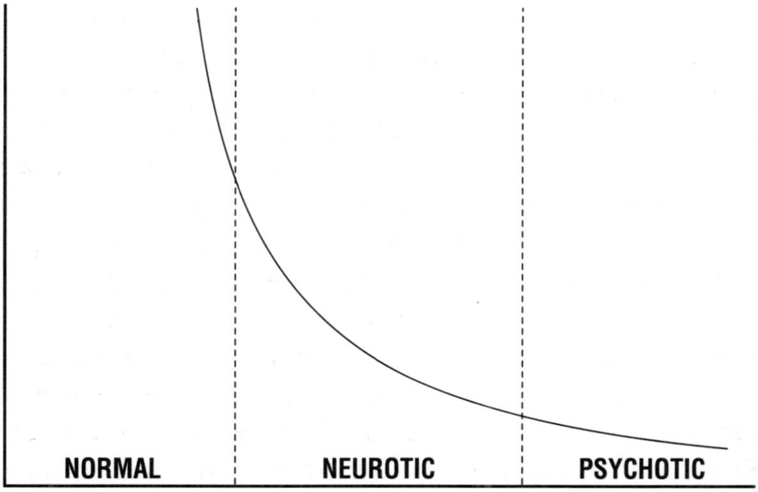

president of the American Psychological Association, who upon examining certain writings that have been sustained culturally over a long period of time, cited the Biblical view of behavior. His different paradigm looked like an "L" shaped curve; suggesting that behavior becomes abnormal through actions that are first identified by an accusing conscience (neurotic) wherein a person begins to worry about his behavior. Then, citing the biblical notion that certain persons have "seared their consciences as with a hot iron" and thereby making it non-operational, the Mowrer paradigm indicates that such a person risks the danger of losing reality orientation (becoming psychotic) when he chooses not to heed the dutiful though accusing conscience and denies that function of the conscience as an essential feedback loop to maintain reality. That person then becomes capable of any sort of behavior, having made a series of decisions which ultimately has caused him to lose self-control. The last state may have become one of no longer being capable of rational behavior, but the person is certainly responsible for the poor choices that brought him to such a point.

The faulty Freudian model has given rise to the notion of false guilt, another erroneous paradigm that was nicely improved upon by Jay Adams in his basic book *Competent To Counsel.*[1] Adams likened the notion of false guilt in the Freudian view to a car with dashboard "idiot lights" which blink red whenever there exists a malfunction in the operating system of an automobile. He likened the dash lights as typical of an accusing conscience. The Freudian therapists, concerned with the notion of false guilt, would suggest that one deal with the guilt rather than the behavior which fosters the guilt and, in Adams' paradigm, would be the person who would take a hammer and smash out the dashboard lights when they flash red, thereby solving the immediate presenting problem. Adams suggests that a better method of healthy response to an accusing conscience is to examine the behaviors that cause the conscience to function as accuser, and in the paradigm he has set forth indicates that a more appropriate response to the dash light's glow is to stop the car, lift up the hood, and attempt to repair the abnormality (behavior) reflected by the warning system (conscience) which is functioning properly.

Seen in this fashion, it becomes obvious that some paradigms are better than others in their ability to represent truth and functionality. In this arena, the game is one of correctness above all else. A faulty world view reaps considerable damage. For example, World War I was supposedly fought to win the world for the sake of democracy, but this paradigm did not take into account that the world may not yet have been ready for democracy, i.e., the inherent cultural maturity of individuals within various countries to comprehend the responsibilities of political freedom without falling into license or anarchy. Such temptations still remain as ongoing possibilities for those in the United States of America who have experienced the product of over two hundred years of democracy.

A view of history sometimes provides measurement as to the truthfulness of our paradigms with piercing revelation about what works and what doesn't. Although mankind has been accused of not learning from history, I am still optimistic that we can learn to shift our paradigms when they are found wanting, and ultimately we will, rejecting as peoples those notions that simply do not work. This apparently holds true for groups and organizations within societies as well.

GUESS HOW MANY BEANS IN THE JAR!

There is an interesting exercise that I have used while teaching graduate coursework in creative leadership at a local southern California university. It is the old "Guess how many beans in the jar" routine. It becomes an indelible object lesson in the benefits of shared perceptions. It works this way:

1. Fill a small, clear glass or plastic jar with a specific number of hard objects, such as marbles, beans, buttons, etc., counting them as you fill the jar.
2. Pass the jar around within your group and ask each person to make a privately determined guess of the correct number of items in the jar, recording their estimation on a piece of paper.
3. Have the individuals in the group pair into twos and come to consensus with their partner, again recording their estimates.
4. Have these pairs join into small groups of fours, again tasked with arriving at consensus, and again writing down their estimates.
5. Continue the process, until you arrive at a total group's consensus of how many items are in the jar, and record the guesstimate.

Then record the range of scores for all to behold, listing the estimates from each step. There will be a greater range of scores gathered from the individualized guesses. The results from pairs will offer a more limited range, and again the guesses in subsequent steps will become more condensed. Usually, the most accurate estimates will come from the final guesstimates of the total group consensus. However, there will sometimes occur some dramatic "skewing" of results due to forceful and dominant personalities at work within a group, concluding more erroneous guesstimates because of their influence within the group.

CREATING MAPS

Paradigms are like maps. They represent the territory, but they are not the territory. Maps are developed by creating many overlays presenting differing perspectives regarding the phenomena being described. Each individual perspective adds to the map, providing detail, and filling in blind spots from other distant views. For this reason, it is essential to include as many of the various viewpoints as possible whenever it is necessary to map out a given situation, valuing each person's individual point of view based on where they sit in life. By being inclusive, there is a greater degree of usefulness in the maps that leaders ultimately establish to navigate a course for the creation of superior solutions to the complex problems with which all are confronted in organizations and contemporary society.

RELATIONSHIPS : PARADIGMS, ATTITUDES, AND BEHAVIORS

William Covey[2], a popular management consultant, humorously shares an illustration that shows the relationship between paradigms and attitudes and behaviors. He tells about a businessman on assignment in Chicago who is mistakenly provided with a map of Detroit as a basic tool for his work in Chicago. Finding that nothing seems to make sense from the beginning of his interaction with events in Chicago based upon the map, he phones his superior and is told to try harder ... in essence, "change your behavior". Still unable to function appropriately, he again contacts his boss, and this time is told to indulge in assimilating the PMA (positive mental attitude) literature, to pump himself up and not become discouraged. He does this, only to find that he is now capable of rushing about Chicago with a giddy smile on his face, but like a lost bus driver, still doesn't know where he is going but is making good time! He has "changed his attitude", but to no avail. He still has a faulty map. Attitudes and behaviors follow from our paradigms. The only effective means to solve the problem is to acquire a proper map ... the right paradigm. With it comes the self-esteem which is appropriately generated from the accomplishment of predetermined goals made possible by a proper and functional view of reality.

PARADIGM SHIFTS

What does it take to "shift a paradigm"?

A mature person has trained himself to think abstractly, analytically and creatively. To think abstractly is to handle adroitly the world of ideas. It has been said that some people think and talk about things, their conversation centered around automobiles, for example. Others focus on people, concerned with nattering on about who did what to whom, the world of eternal afternoon television soaps. Then there are those whose thought life focuses on the world of ideas, on concepts, and their consequences. To think analytically implies a disciplined mind that can function logically, discerning the difference between emotions and rationality, not prone to being hooked by manipulative marketeers preying on subconscious emotional seductions. To think creatively is to respond with the blending of a deep sense of caring and with a mind free from constraints of norms, unhindered from concerns of fear and guilt, daring to courageously confront the gaps between "what is" and "what should be." A fully developed person will have a mind disciplined and equipped to function abstractly, analytically, and creatively. Such a person can provide the insight to present a better way of perceiving a situation, and communicating that better way in acceptable terms to those who may benefit by the paradigm shift. Such a person can change the world.

Victor Frankl has been such a person. Perhaps you know his story. It is the account of a Jewish psychiatrist who chose to remain in Nazi Germany rather than escape with his colleagues when Adolph Hitler was arousing hatred for Jewish ethnicity. Eventually thrown into Auschwitz, he discovered a profound truth that has been remarkably communicated since his repatriation and subsequent writings as a post WWII educator and therapist. Frankl learned that the most essential characteristic of being human was the power to chose to respond to any situation on the basis of internal integrity, not on the basis of the stimulation. He found that he did not have to respond in like manner to the hatred and loathing towards his captors and tormentors. Rather than descending to their level of understanding and behavior, he could chose to retain his human liberty by selecting always how he would respond to anything that was thrown at him. He chose not to allow others to control his inner life. That was his domain solely to handle as he saw fit. His autobiography, *Man's Search for Meaning*, documenting his experience and growth, has become standard reading for those who have become discouraged and depressed by environmental, social and psychological bombardments.

Frankl provided a life-breathed example of a paradigm-shift that others who chose to follow may also experience for themselves. When a person realizes that he always has the choice to respond as he wants to a given stimulation, he is forever free. He is beyond manipulation, either by others or himself. For example, it is a profound realization to understand that we can always respond in love, if we chose, to any kind of circumstance that is presented to us.

This understanding of paradigm creation, development, and change or "shift" also brings with it the realization that, while our maps can become better and better, at best they become very useful but they are only representations of truth; many sided, multifaceted truth, of which no mere mortal seems to have exclusivity or over-arching encompassment. This is the nature of the philosophy of science, ever searching for better ways of beholding reality, applied at the level of everyman.

THE POLYTROPHIC LEADERSHIP CONTINUUM PARADIGM

The next chapter sets forth a leadership continuum based on certain Biblical values, norms, and concepts, such as maturity as the goal of leadership. It also takes into consideration the building blocks of personality development discussed in the preceding chapter.

The paradigm is simply a better map than that which has been offered by other examiners of leadership behavior, providing insight for those concerned with how their own leadership behaviors and choices can be improved.

Notes

1. Adams, Jay E. *Competent to Counsel.* Grand Rapids: Baker Book House, 1970.
2. Covey, Stephen R. *The Seven Habits of Highly Effective People.* New York: Simon and Schuster, 1989.

CHAPTER SIX

The Polytrophic Leadership Continuum Model

One person may best respond to the most uncompromising challenge, while another needs patient encouragement. One is told that his life already approximates in pattern to what God is wanting him to be; but another may be told bluntly that despite all his religious profession, he is at heart a "child of evil." Once we grasp the underlying principle of love in action touching human lives in various states of awareness and development, we can begin to understand why so many different things were said to so many different people. —J. B. Phillips in *God Our Contemporary*

As we have indicated, people grow through various stages of development. Scholars list many scenarios with a broad variety of substages, but for the sake of simplicity, the model set forth here will focus on just the five basic stages already identified: infancy, childhood, adolescence, young adult, and mature. There are certainly other identifiable stages depending on the observer's perspective, but these five are suggested for the sake of clarity and expediency. In the illustration below, we see the correlation between leadership style and developmental stage coupled with their respective characteristics and orientation.

LEADERSHIP STYLE	AUTOCRATIC	PATERNALISTIC	PARTISAN	DEMOCRATIC	PARTICIPATIVE
DEVELOPMENTAL STAGE	INFANCY	CHILDHOOD	ADOLESCENCE	YOUNG ADULT	MATURE
CHARACTERISTIC	DEPENDENCY	EXPLORATION	EXPERIMENTATION	APPLICATION	ACTUALIZATION
ORIENTATION	SELF	FAMILY	GROUP	SOCIETY	WORLD VIEW

The model indicates that there are trade-offs that occur quite naturally between the development stage and the five common leadership styles. A review of the various stages and their attending leadership styles, while not exhaustive, suggests that the matching of "leadership styles" and "follower needs" occurs on the continuum. Each seeks out the other and is comfortable once found. Like mating calls, communications between leaders and followers reveal each other's needs and predispositions, and relationships are consummated, some are transient, some are enduring. The leader styles towards the left of the continuum work most effectively for those who can assume high degrees of control. This control and authority is progressively more shared between leader and follower as one movs to the right of the continuum. Task complexity also increases progressively from left to right, i.e., groups are capable of simple tasks on the left of the continuum, where they are limited by the leader's resources. Toward the right, groups are capable of completing complex tasks in response to complex needs.

Characteristically, the INFANCY stage is described as the stage of DEPENDENCY, noted by structure-seeking, authority orientation, inner-directedness, fixed labeling, helplessness, adaptation, desire for instant gratification, and a general limitation to accomplishment of only simple tasks.

The CHILDHOOD stage is described as a stage of EXPLORATION, and noted by the needs for security, and the characteristics of dependency, limit-testing, sudden growth, skill identification, personality formulation, and the basic processes of socialization.

ADOLESCENCE is described as a stage of EXPERIMENTATION. It is characterized as: peer-oriented, outer-directed, fad conscious, willing to substitute alternative schemes for security. It is a time to resolve the issues of authority, skills/habit formulation, individual identity development and the tendency to conform to peer influences.

The YOUNG ADULT stage is depicted as a stage of APPLICATION characterized by: trial and error, creative but often unrealistic visions, idealism and openness. It is normative, abstract, goal-oriented and aggressive.

The MATURITY stage, considered more operational than actual, is the stage of ACTUALIZATION. It is described as phenomenologically perceptive, (i.e., seeing situations and individuals as unique). It is spontaneous, creative, inner-directed, communicative, aware of the semantic bargain, results-oriented, sensitive, assured, and capable of complex tasks.

The AUTOCRATIC leader, as a style, is characterized by the type of person who pushes his control to the limits. He is quick to provide personal agenda, structure, direction, task definition and tends to dominate the follower-groups. This leader can be understood as benevolent when his behavior reflects a response to follower needs. However, when this leader becomes more concerned with his own status, power and control, as opposed to task facilitation and individual group member's growth and development, he becomes AUTHORITARIAN. This phenomenon has been addressed in a previous chapter because it is so recurrent.

The PATERNALISTIC leadership style, is similar to the autocratic due to its degree of leader dependence developed. The paternalistic leader is one who has "an iron hand in a velvet glove." Whether paternalistic or maternalistic (as either one may assume this role), these leaders, envision themselves as nurturing and providing structure, support, direction and agenda so as to maintain a sense of familial community. There exists a danger in developing this subtle sense of "patronization," for it readily becomes offensively condescending in nature. Studies indicate that due to excessive dependence on the leader, there is an inherent collapse of organizations and groups whenever either the AUTOCRATIC or PATERNALISTIC leader is removed from the group.

The PARTISAN style exists when there is an emphasis on comparing, usually competitively, this group with other similar groups. The partisan leader's motivation is riveted on concerns for the marketing of this particular group/organization/party; "my group is better than your group." This leader is engaged in a sort of popularity contest or "one-upmanship" intended to maintain a supposed superiority. His *esprit de corps* marks his personality as typical of the kind to which the high school year book is generally dedicated. But he provides enough structure for group members to feel free to experiment, having an identity with the group which provides needed security.

The DEMOCRATIC leadership style is characterized by the leader who is concerned with the appropriate utilization of human resources in a manner conducive to maximum input from group members. This leader obviously implies dependence upon a certain amount of maturity within the membership, and relies on the coordinated efforts of each contributor, sometimes resulting in group accomplishments that display the lowest common denominator in terms of vision, creativity, and quality rather than the highest!

PARTICIPATIVE leaders are differentiated by their willingness to share their authority in all group and organizational tasks. Devoid of ego-assertive needs, this leader is most willing to share any group role, being comfortable when the group decides what to do and how to do it. Similar to circumstances of the democratic leadership style, success is dependent on the resources of the group. The participative leader, however, differs greatly in that he draws to himself spontaneous self-starters who may have broad capacities for sustained and complex task completion.

The relationships and normal trade-offs between leaders and followers hold true in terms of the polytrophic leadership continuum paradigm even when applied to other dynamics of human developmental such as the six areas of personality development, i.e., social, mental-educational, physical, spiritual, family and financial growth. For example, a person's pattern of spiritual development will also go through these same stages of infancy, childhood, adolescence, young adulthood and, hopefully, maturity. Persons in each stage will, in turn, be influenced substantially by people who assume the attending leadership styles as they proceed through the various stages. The same dynamics appear to hold for cultures and societies as well, being profoundly influenced by leaders who function in roles that fit the circumstances and possessing appropriate styles of leadership.

Could an Idi Amin arise if the potential of dependency didn't exist in Uganda? Certainly the old communistic revolutionary theorem which states "Rub raw the wounds of discontent" is applied and unrest is generated creating situations of dependency and regressions to stages of infancy by the people. Then, with the ensuing turmoil, the environment is prepared for strongman leadership which is "authoritarian" by definition. There is an old tabloid saying that "the times call the man." For the unwitting, this can be tragically true.

CROSS-FERTILIZATIONS

In the paradigm, cross-fertilization of styles and needs certainly do occur, but the results are neither enduring nor satisfying. Thus, for

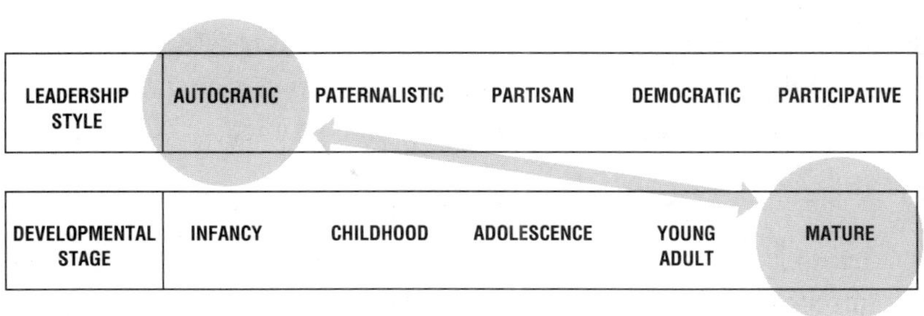

example, when the autocrat attempts activity with mature individuals and groups, he is normally destined to experience alienation, his style being perceived as that of an increasingly unpalatable surrogate god.

The other class of cross-fertilization, i.e., participative leadership involvement with immature groups and individuals, is equally ineffectual. Match-ups with those in the childhood stage breeds chaos, because their immaturity reflects an inability to realize what behaviors would be appropriate in a given situation. People who are childlike simply do not have the awareness to make astute decisions, and are incapable of implementing those that they do make.

Also, those less functionally mobile in the infancy stage respond

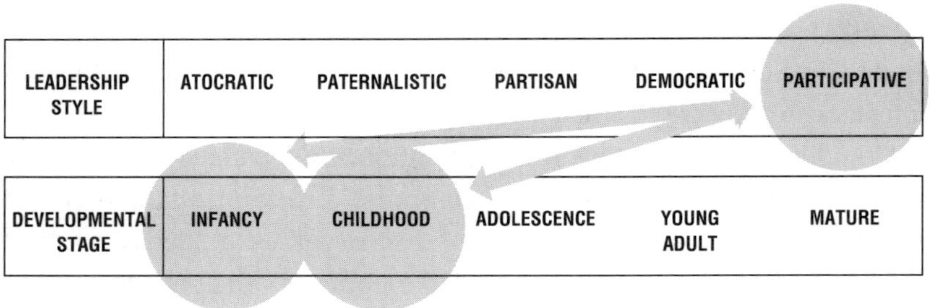

with hostility to the leader who chooses not to provide the desirable structure on which they depend. Their hostility many times will take the form of an attack on the legitimacy of the leadership that does not meet their expectations. These immature followers are, however, distinguished by their utter incapacity to fend for themselves and while they are displeasured by the leader who gives them too much freedom to the point of rejection, they unfortunately tend to go from the frying pan of one rejected leader into the the fires of the next leader. The situation is similar to the constant turnover in marketing oriented corporations which frequently replace managers, but never recognize and deal with the inherent causes of the organizational problem.

THE POLYTROPHIC LEADER

The understanding of normally occurring trade-offs along the continuum provide the case for the POLYTROPHIC Leader. The word is derived from the Greek word, "poly," meaning "many," and "trophos," the root word for "to nourish," hence, "to nourish in many ways." The polytroph effectively leads at every point on the continuum. He becomes all things to all men.

If the maturity of the individual is valued in an organization or group, then leadership styles become a function of that value!

POLYTROPHIC LEADERSHIP

LEADERSHIP STYLE	ATOCRATIC	PATERNALISTIC	PARTISAN	DEMOCRATIC	PARTICIPATIVE

DEVELOPMENTAL STAGE	INFANCY	CHILDHOOD	ADOLESCENCE	YOUNG ADULT	MATURE

The Polytrophic Leader becomes the silly putty of leadership by assuming any other style necessary for the development of the individual and group as well as getting the task completed. This is the person who can work within the entire continuum of human relationships. Polytrophic leaders are supremely "people persons." They care, and they communicate their deepening caring to others found in all levels of growth and maturity. Significantly, polytrophic leaders become rock-solid in their espousal and implementation of values that develop others to maturity. This overt commitment to human growth and development demands, however, that they acquire a variety of methods and means to carry out that task. They become, then, as flexible in how they influence others to grow as they are inflexible that such growth must occur.

On measures of Task/People concern, polytrophic leaders score high both in influencing productivity and developing morale.[1] Polytrophic leaders are characterized not only by their flexibility, but by their ability to risk, communicate, grow with their groups, disdain power needs, lead through others, and model congruency. ("Congruency" occurs when a person's thinking, emotions and language are superimposed. For example, when one says, "I feel angry towards you when you mess up an assignment.") Of necessity, they have acquired skills of keying on others, responding to their needs as a frame of reference, and guiding others to predetermined outcomes.[2]

Many contemporary organizational and societal needs require complex solutions, and polytrophic leadership offers the greatest promise of developing resources to create appropriate solutions which may be as complex as necessary to meet the identified needs. Another circumstance calling for this approach is impact of change brought on by technological advancements in communication, electronic technology, travel and information systems. These factors compound the need for enlightened, flexible and caring leaders.

THE POLYTROPH AND LEADER GROWTH

It must be acknowledged that many leaders do not grow. There is much to be said for the idea of the leader-learner. Unfortunately, some who have aspired to leadership status feel that they have "arrived" once commissioned to a leader role and their pride of accomplishment does not leave room for additional growth and development. Then too, much of recent counsel regarding leadership suggests that a person find his leadership style and then find an environment in which to exercise it. However, to the degree that a leader fixates on a given leadership style, he limits his influence upon various segments of followers on the continuum.

It should be realized that the most natural phenomenon is for people to "fixate" at a leadership style. That is, they select a format with which they are comfortable and attempt to shoehorn all situations into their selected mode of operation. Of course, this is short-sighted, but more than the impracticality of limiting leadership influence to those narrow bands on the continuum where they are effective, these stagnated leaders raise a whole new issue reflected by their apparent absence of love. The authentic Christian knows that love is a fruit of the Holy Spirit's control over personality. In a real and genuine sense, to love as Christ loves is thereby a supernatural phenomenon ... but it is not only within the grasp of all believers, it is the norm commanded for those who have been redeemed. And just as a person has to make a conscious choice to receive salvation and the indwelling Spirit, so he has to make the conscious choice to love others as Christ loves. And just as bald reason indicates the necessity and benefits to work the entire continuum, the capacity to do so issues from the choice and desire to love one another.

Another consideration for polytrophism lies in the realization that rarely is there a group of homogeneous persons such that a leader is not forced to change styles for facilitation within a group. Also, every leader can expect to discover that each person's development occurs at different rates with regard to growth physically, mentally, spiritually, economically, socially, and in terms of family relationships. Some may need constant encouragement, while others may respond best to the kick in the rear. A mature leader is capable of making these proper choices of servant-leadership for the benefit of others and the sake of the task when necessary. This is the basic shortcoming of the person who becomes authoritarian. He lacks the ability to love genuinely, or grow with his group. More concerned with his own needs for status, power and control than he is with developing others to maturity, he fails to lead effectively because of his psychological and spiritual myopia.

Notes

1. Pheiffer and Jones, 1974.
2. Sperry and Hess, 1974

STATUS, POWER AND CONTROL: SOUTH OF THE BORDER

It seems that there was a late influx of players wishing to play in the "Latin American Open Golf Tournament" which shall, for courtesy sake, go further unnamed. They had missed the registration deadline, relying instead on the advice of influential persons who were in leadership within the LAPGA, and who guaranteed that they could get them into the tournament at the last moment if necessary.

This behavior is typical of those who rely on status rather than on effective planning and management policies to get things accomplished. It represents the "good old boy network." The head of the Latin American Golf Federation pleaded his case to me as the "contracted tournament director" to allow them to play because if they were denied it would open a recently healed wound in the relationship between the federation and the PGA. Not coincidentally, it would reinforce his own status, power, and control to be able to take credit for resolving a crisis, even if it were indirectly his own creation. It would be an affirmation of his "macho" image to sway the situation with timely intervention. His power of personality would overcome the obstacles and enable him to assume the role of "basic power broker." During any ensuing crises, everyone would know whom to enlist for relief. And he would be reaffirmed as the man with the status and power to rescue all in the situation. And on, and on, and on. This game he would play was preferable to "planning the work and working the plan," which did not offer the emotional and political payoffs that some culturally acceptable methods afford.

Letting the additional competitors play created another set of problems. The field had already been overfilled, and the tournament was scheduled for play only ten days before the winter solstice, providing us with some of the shortest daylight hours of the year. There simply was no more room to play! And at the site there was only one golf course. Eighteen holes. No place for additional play. Attempting to accommodate the extra twelve players would incorporate at least three additional tee times, and with the normal six to eight minutes between groups, would add another half hour to the schedule at least. It simply wasn't possible.

My creative solution was to insert as many players as possible, filling up any missed tee times with players considered "alternates" and, as a last resort, inserting additional tee times between the cross-over as we implemented starting players on both the front and back nines. It would be extremely tight, but worth the gamble "to keep peace between the factions."

As a competitor, I chose an early starting time from the tenth tee so that an early finish would enable me to be free to cope with any emergencies that might crop up. I was putting out on the fourth hole when it happened. I heard bands playing, and I wondered about the sounds, something like a college football game taking place nearby, but it was incongruous with the Latin American scenario. I dismissed the phenomenon and concentrated on my game. Making the turn by the clubhouse, one of my management team informed me that the officials of the federation had taken the liberty of holding an inauguration of the tournament on the first tee, the ceremony including both the mayor and the governor. With them were other eminent personalities, each giving welcoming orations to accompany the dignitaries of the golf federation. By the time it concluded, the golf course had been tied up for over a half hour, with foursomes backing up one on top of another.

I groaned. Then I groaned again when I had to halt play on account of darkness with approximately ten groups still on the course. They would have to finish at the crack of dawn the next morning, then scurry for their starting time for day two. For some, it meant starting at dawn, completing three holes, and then teeing off directly for round two. What a way to run an airline! It was surprising how few became angry at the arrangements.

The "inauguration" could have been accomplished during the two preceding days during the pro-am part of the competition without any compounding consequences. It could have been done at one of the festivities surrounding the affair in the evening. There were many other alternatives. But if status and power is your thing, what better way to assert authority than to hold up the entire tournament while taking bows in front of one's honorable constituency? Concerns for task completion took a back seat to concerns for reinforcing status; a far, far back seat. Concern for the individuals who were attempting to compete, caught by darkness, interrupting their competitive bearing, and forcing a farcical second day schedule for them, was overshadowed by the need to display the reflections of relational status with the governing leaders.

CALVIN AND HOBBES By Bill Watterson

CHAPTER SEVEN

The Polytroph and Organizational Growth

THE PROBLEM OF CONFLICT

The Group Development Model[1] describes four stages in the evolution of a group. Each of the four phases has two major dimensions: personal relations and task functions. Jones concluded that the progress along these two paths is parallel and interrelated. The Polytroph becomes the means of optimum group development, capable of nurturing organizational growth through the four stages to organizational effectiveness indicated in the paradigm.

The personal relations dimension of the model encompasses all the interrelationships that people develop and sustain in the group—their feelings, expectations, commitments, assumptions, paradigms, and problems with one another. The four stages of PERSONAL RELATIONS correlate with the development of the identity and functions of a group from the personal orientations of the members. The four stages of TASK FUNCTIONS correlate with the progress of a group in understanding and accomplishing its work. As the group moves through the personal relations and task functions stages simultaneously, the progress and setbacks in one dimension influence the behavior and progress in the other.

The Leadership Continuum paradigm also parallels the four stages of organizational growth as indicated in the following descriptions of each stage.

STAGE ONE

In Stage One, group members are highly dependent in their personal relations. They rely on safe patterned behavior and look to the group leader for guidance and direction. In their task functions, the members are getting oriented to the task. Discussion centers around defining the scope of the task, how to approach it, etc. Stage One is inclusive of the two Leadership Continuum trade-offs of Autocratic/Infancy and Paternalistic-maternalistic/Childhood stages, reflecting its dependent and exploratory nature at this initial stage of development.

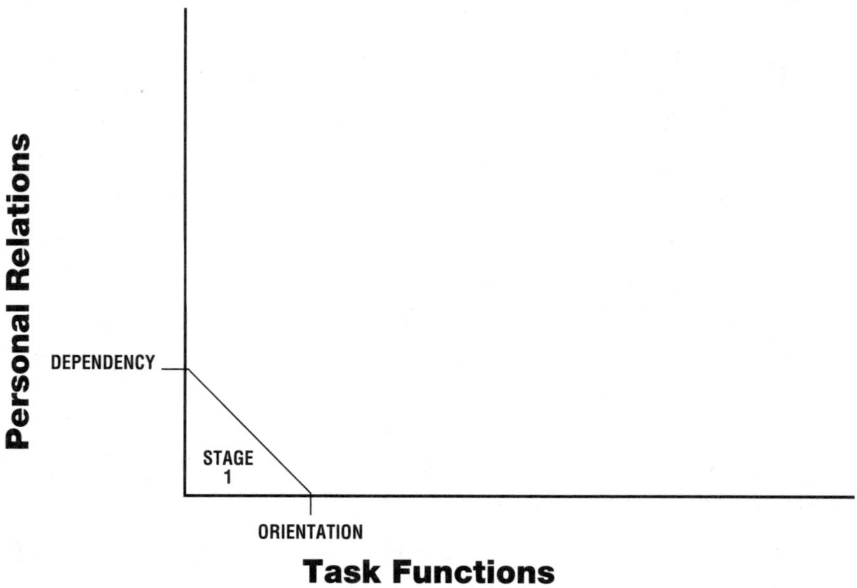

STAGE TWO

As the group members attempt to organize for the task at Stage Two, conflict inevitably occurs in their personal relationships. As group members begin to exercise individual authority to carry out

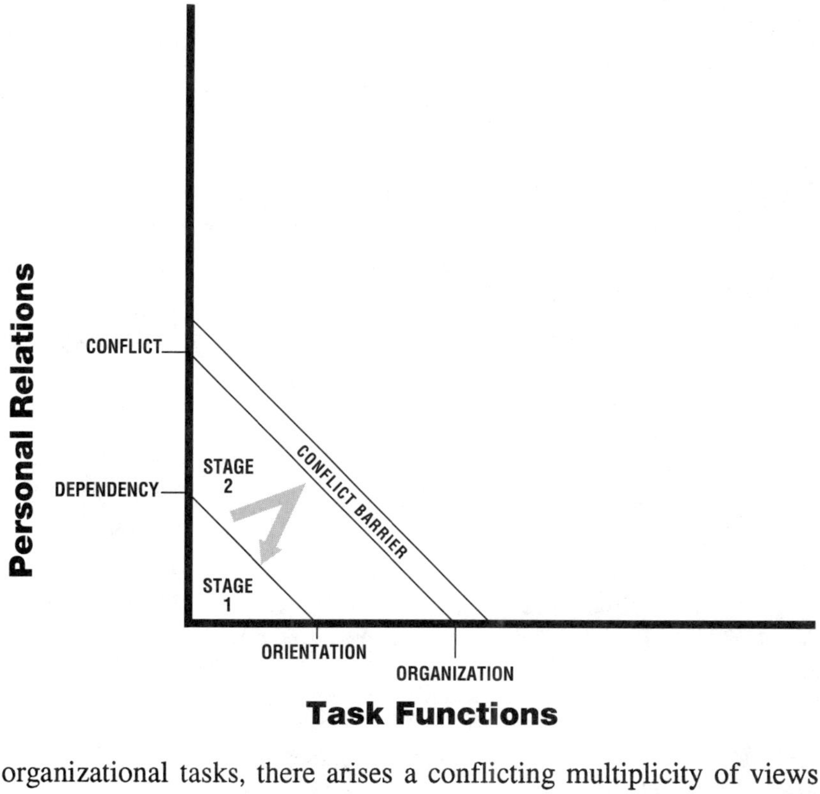

organizational tasks, there arises a conflicting multiplicity of views concerning methods/means, etc. Like a jury in deliberation, individuals have to bend and mold their feelings, ideas, attitudes, perhaps even shifting paradigms and beliefs to suit the group organization. Although conflicts may or may not surface as group issues, they do exist. If the group does not have conflict resolution skills embodied in its membership, and conflict does arise openly, the progress of group development is set back to Stage One again, depending on leadership to again orient and provide basic reorganization. It is not unusual for another set of leaders to attempt to penetrate this huge conflict barrier, supplanting the former leadergroup when they fail to produce the required results.

Stage Two parallels the Partisan/Adolescent Stage of the Leadership Continuum Model, as it applies to group development. Organizationally speaking, there are similar characteristics which describe the group's identity as "Adolescent" at this stage due to its volatile and experimental nature.

STAGE THREE

The major task function of Stage Three is the data flow between group members—they share feelings, solicit and give feedback to one another, and explore actions related to the task. When members begin to know and identify with one another, the level of trust in their personal relationships contributes to the development of group cohesion. Normally, the successful resolution of conflict while keeping group

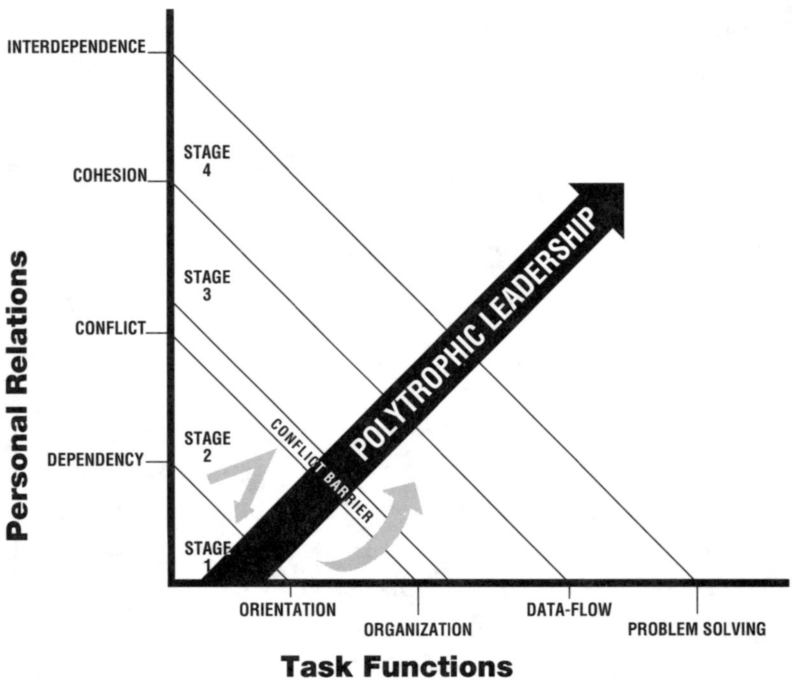

norms and values intact breeds an esprit de corps, a sense of enthusiasm and cooperation that is felt by group members signifying their ability to overcome significant obstacles on their way to group fulfillment. If this stage of data flow and cohesion is reached, group interactions are characterized by openness and sharing of information on both a personal and task level. They feel good about being part of an effective group. They also have learned the skills of integrating unique individual differences among members, building on their strengths while coping with and shoring up their weaknesses.

Stage Three parallels the Democratic/Young Adult trade-off as described in the Leadership Continuum paradigm, emphasizing the practical and applied outworking of the group's development. They are highly functional, know what they are about and why, but have not yet reached the position of accumulating a history of consistent accomplishments.

Since much conflict is inevitable because different people have different viewpoints, values, paradigms and beliefs, the goal of a group is not so much to eliminate conflict but to **manage** it. Conflict is essentially healthy, breeding creativity when handled constructively. New ideas and new learnings result when exploring differences openly. Conflict becomes destructive and injurious to group members when mismanaged, occurring when the wrong strategies are used, or hidden agenda disallows the proper identification of the nature of the conflict.

There are five common ways of dealing with organizational conflict. Any one method of dealing with conflict will not apply to all situations or all personalities. The leader in a group must consider when to employ what style, and with whom. If a leader has used one method successfully, he may use it to excess, fixating on a conflict-resolution style in the same manner as fixating on a leadership style....with the same disastrous results. Learning about the alternative means of handling conflict gives us a wider choice of actions to employ in any given situation and makes us better able to tailor the response to the situation.

1. Denial or Withdrawal

With this approach, a person attempts to "get rid of" conflict by denying that it exists. He simply refuses to acknowledge it. Usually, however, the conflict does not "go away"; it grows to the point where it becomes all but unmanageable. When the issue or the timing is not critical, denial may be the most productive way of dealing with conflict on a temporary basis.

2. Suppression or Smoothing Over

"We run a happy ship here." "Nice people don't fight." A person using suppression plays down differences and does not recognize the positive aspects of handling the conflict openly. Again, the source of the conflict rarely goes away. Suppression may, however, be employed when it is more important to preserve a relationship than to deal with an insignificant issue at the price of conflict.

3. Power or Dominance

Power is often used to settle differences. The source of the power used may be one's authority or position (including referral to "the system," higher supervision, and so on). Power may take the form of a majority (as in voting) or a persuasive minority. Power strategies, however, result in winners and losers, and the losers do not support a final decision in the same way that winners do. Future meetings of a group may be marred by the conscious or unconscious renewal of the struggle previously "settled" by the use of power. In some instances, especially where other forms of handling conflict are clearly inappropriate, power is effective. Voting is used in national elections, for example, and "the law" applies equally to all.

4. Compromise or Negotiation

Although often regarded as a virtue in our culture, compromise ("You give a little, I'll give a little, and we'll meet each other halfway") has some serious drawbacks. Bargaining often causes both sides to assume an inflated position, since they are aware that they are going to have to "give a little" and want to buffer the loss. The compromise solution may be watered down or weakened to the point where it will not be effective. There is often little real commitment by any of the parties. Also, a wise person will know what issues are considered non-negotiables and which issues are negotiable. Yet there are times when compromise makes sense, such as when resources are limited or it is necessary to forestall a win-lose situation.

5. Integration or Collaboration

This approach requires that all parties to the conflict recognize the abilities and expertise of the others. Each individual's position is well prepared, but the emphasis of the group is on trying to solve the problem at hand, rather than on defending particular positions or factions. Everyone fully expects to modify his original views as the group's work progresses. Ultimately, the best of the group's thinking will emerge. The assumption is that the whole of the group effort exceeds the sum of the individuals members' contributions. If this approach is allowed to become an either/or settlement, or if the conflict is resolved—due to lack of time, money, or understanding—by a form of power, the final decision will suffer accordingly.[2]

Integration assumes the existence both of the Holy Spirit and agape love as a basis for relationship and resolution, and is the most demanding, but satisfactory method for conflict resolution in keeping with the worth and dignity of each person. James again provides a sound foundation for its utilization:

> The wisdom that comes from heaven is first of all pure; then peace-loving, considerate, submissive, full of mercy and good fruit, impartial and sincere. (James 3:17)

STAGE FOUR

If group members are able to evolve organizationally to Stage Four, their capacity, range, and depth of personal relations expand to true interdependence. In this stage, people can work singly, in subgroups, or as a total unit with equal facility. Their roles and authorities dynamically adjust to the changing needs of the group, individuals, and the sociological, economic, and spiritual milieu in which they operate. They can interact creatively upon their environment because their task functions become genuinely problem-solving, leading to optimal solutions and optimum group development. At this stage the group represents an organization that functions like an organism, interacting positively with its environment.

Stage Four groups have arrived, and they parallel the Participative/Mature trade-off from the Leadership Continuum. Individuals in groups at this stage function as true professionals. They bespeak authenticity, consistency, excellence, and accomplishment. What you see is what you get from almost all dimensions of organizations led in this way. These individuals comprehend the meaning and application of Polytrophic leadership.

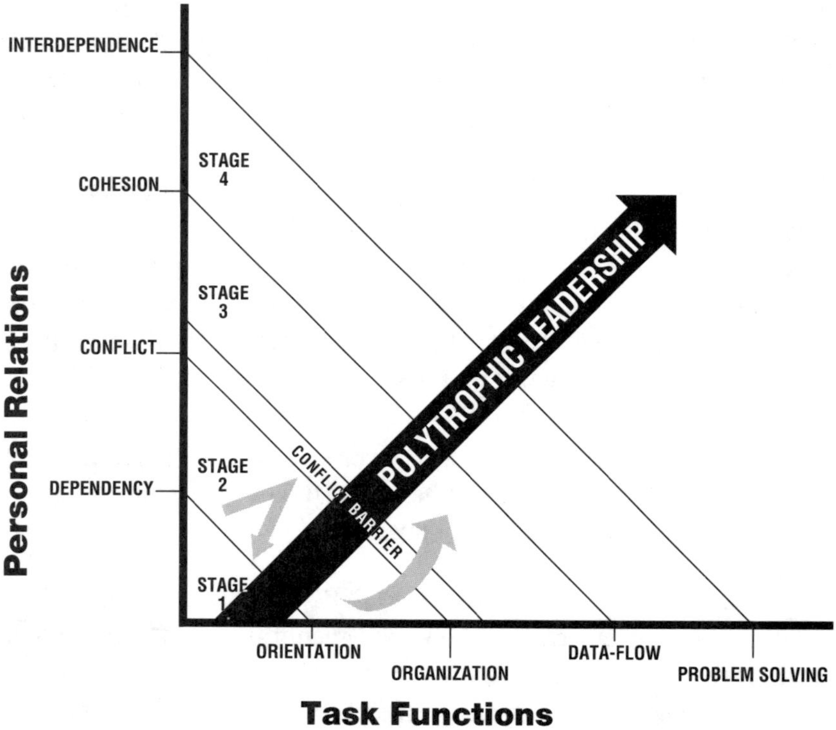

Notes

1. Boshear, Walton C., and Karl G. Albrecht. *Understanding People: Models and Concepts.* La Jolla, CA: University Associates, Inc., 1977.
2. Pfeiffer, J. William, PhD and John E. Jones, PhD, Eds. *The 1976 Annual Handbook for Group Facilitators.* LaJolla, CA: University Associates, Inc., 1976.

LEADERSHIP AND THE LOCAL CHURCH

There is a local community church which was pastored by the same person for over thirty-three years. As a controller/autocratic leader, he carried out the duties of the church in a paternalistic fashion, but the iron hand was always in the velvet glove. When retirement became inevitable, he chose to hand-pick his successor, a man from outside of the church staff, having a similar theological stance and style as his own. When the new man came aboard at his urging, the old pastor remained involved as "pastor emeritus" thus enabling him to continue to perform many ministerial functions for the congregation. The new man, in search for his own constituency, instigated greater participation from the congregation.

As a community church there had been a mix of theological experiences including a range of charismatic believers who were some of the first to respond to the new pastor's opportunities for greater involvement and expression. However, with their new freedom, responsibilities, and increased visibility, "praying in tongues" became a threat for the majority of parishioners who did not share that cognizance, and the ensuing conflict resulted in a mass exodus of about fifty of the younger and enthusiastic charismatic couples from the fellowship. The new pastor justified the departure as a crisis of identity which, although not a necessary rationale for disunion in the past, now required a purging of these people.

Subsequent conflicts also resulted in various subgroups within the church deciding to leave "en masse." After about the fourth such exodus, a vote of confidence was requested by a disgruntled segment of the membership that remained. Giving had degenerated, creative financial management strategies were being utilized, and there existed a general attitude that things were not right. Many people had withdrawn from active participation, and there were many who felt that it was time for the new pastor to resign.

The meeting for the vote was attended by people not seen at the church for months, and in some instances years. The debate became lively, emotional, and for some speakers heated. Some members described how dear the church was to them through the years, gathering support for their side of the dilemma. Both sides were vociferous and seemingly adamant about the role of the pastor. Finally, the assistant pastor commandeered the podium, and told the congregation that if they didn't back the pastor, the entire staff would resign and they would not have anyone to run the church for them. "Then see who will run this church!" were his concluding words. It was a bald threat! Certainly the substance that would guarantee dismissal if done in a secular business setting. But no one acknowledged the threat as such. They simply folded in to the demands of the assistant pastor and staff and voted narrowly for the continued ministry. Another group left the church.

The church still goes through the motions. But there is no fire. Growth has remained nonexistent. The staff is entrenched with the remaining members. Surrounding churches continue to grow, but the community church maintains the status quo.

UPDATE: Eight years after assuming the pastorate, the senior pastor has resigned. Distressed that the church is going no place, he laments that he has never experienced such a number of resignations from the elderboard in all of his other pastorates put together. "This church is run like a chaplaincy, where the pastor is the appointed responsible person. Everybody else does nothing," he states.

He freely admits that he had thinned out the congregation as much as he felt he should, but he believes that these people just do not have leadership capacities; they readily run from the congregation whenever there is conflict. The assistant pastor is planning to start a new church in another geographic area under the auspices of a different church denomination.

CALVIN & HOBBES

"Will the witness please tell the court exactly how long he's known the accused?"

CHAPTER EIGHT

Leader Sins

QUARRELS, CONFLICT, ALIENATION, DIVIDED HOUSES

"None of these has been lost ... except the son of perdition, Judas who betrayed Jesus."

How could Judas Iscariot do such a thing? What on earth could he have been thinking? Betraying the Son of God! Surely he witnessed His power. He knew of the raising of Lazarus, the blind receiving their sight, the lame walking. All sorts of sicknesses healed. Jesus walking on the water. The feeding of the five thousand with a youngster's lunch. He saw what Moses longed to see.

Yet Jesus would say of him, *"It would have been better for that man if he had not been born."* The ultimate tragedy among the disciples.

Judas seemingly took a calculated risk. There are many who think that Judas' actions were taken in order to force the Lord Jesus into taking command of the events surrounding himself and the nation, thus emerging as the conquering messiah yearned for by many. The problem of Judas was that he saw God in man's image. Drastically misunderstanding, he tried to force God into his own paradigm and paid the supreme price for his choice to **use** the Lord rather than **trust** him. It was a question of who was to be in control. Is this not the ultimate question for all of us?

BREAKING THE CONFLICT BARRIER: UNDERSTANDING SIN

When group and organizational growth is understood more fully, the paradigms shed light on identifying certain problems that always exist in group, organizational and interpersonal behaviors. There is one enormous, obvious, and grossly misunderstood basic cause of conflict. The Bible identifies it as "sin." Unfortunately, our contemporary age has not retained a solid biblical understanding of the concept, and its use has become staid, and warped by contemporary society and churches alike. It should come as no surprise that local churches are enculturated by the media, opinion makers, social mores, and other outside influences.

In his classic work entitled *Whatever Became of Sin?*, psychoanalyst Karl Menninger writes about the avoidance of the word.

The very word "sin," which seems to have disappeared, was a proud word. It was a strong word, an ominous and serious word. It described a central point in every civilized human being's life plan and life style. But the word went away. It has almost disappeared—the word, along with the notion. Why? Doesn't anyone sin anymore? Doesn't anyone believe in sin?[1]

The wrongfulness of the sinful act lies not merely in its nonconformity, its departure from the accepted, appropriate way of behavior, but in an implicitly aggressive quality—a ruthlessness, a hurting, a breaking away from God and from the rest of humanity, a partial alienation, or act of rebellion. Sin has a willful, defiant, or disloyal quality; someone is defied or offended or hurt. The willful disregard or sacrifice of the welfare of others for the welfare or satisfaction of the self is an essential quality of the concept sin.[2]

The New Testament word *hamartia* has as its basic meaning the idea of failure, as its earliest classical Greek meaning carried the notion of "missing the mark" as a spear missing the target. Although the word became vested with much more sinister baggage in the New Testament usages, it is wise not to overlook the heritage of the concept as it applies to contemporary situations and persons. When people get wrapped up in themselves, defining their own values and beliefs from some inner system devoid of God, they are again "missing the mark" profoundly. There is a deep disappointment in the heart of the Polytroph when he recognizes the manner in which personal choices can blunt God's purposes in human lives. The leadership of love is always vulnerable to heartbreak when others select sin rather than growth towards maturity, meaning, purpose and fulfillment. Having so much potential unrealized is always a sad situation, ultimately harming the self as well as others.

The understanding of sin includes the realization that it is a power which has man in its grasp; the true opiate of the people. "So basic is the hold of sin over a man that sin is not merely an external power which exercises sway over a man; it has got into the very fibre and center and heart of his being until it occupies him, as an enemy occupies an occupied territory."[3]

In Augustine's Confessions, he tells a story about stealing a huge load of pears from a nearby pear-tree, enjoying not so much the pears, but doing with impunity what was forbidden, with a dim similitude of omnipotence. Sin certainly provides perceptions of personal power, even if short-lived and self-defeating. It represents another alternative to the person who, lacking in a sense of self-worth, desires instant gratification through a counterfeit of freedom and power. Sinful choices and behavior are always entangling, not ultimately liberating. When an individual is enticed by subtle appeals to power or pleasure, and succumb to those enticements, it is difficult for him to determine the normal consequences of behavior, so blinding is the power of sin.

DIATREPHES REVISITED

Diatrephes was a leader in the church, but he had what Organizational Axiotherapists would now cite as "control-needs," a form of ugly sin. It metastasizes from the sin of doubt, and is typical of one who, because of unattended insecurity, still has concerns for himself and has to control situations to his satisfaction, rendering him useless to the kingdom of God. The sin of Diatrephes was that he always sought the uppermost place.

One of the New Testament words for leadership is derived from the person who gives direction to a ship like a helmsman, steering, making the necessary decisions for its path and destiny as a ship's captain. Diatrephes' problem, akin to many contemporary Christian leaders and pastors, comes from the notion that they are the owners of the ship, not just stewards or managers who serve for the real owner. They have fallen in love with the role of their positions, that love replacing their first love for the Lord, and forcefully deny access to anyone else who may genuinely desire to exercise individual gifts or become part of the organization's leadership resources. John's third letter (9-10.) describes John's handling of him,

> *I wrote to the church, but Diatrephes, who loves to be first, will have nothing to do with us. So if I come, I will call attention to what he is doing, gossiping maliciously about us. Not satisfied with that, he refuses to welcome brothers. He also stops those who want to do so and puts them out of the church.*

In this familiar process, Diatrephes is seen as a leader who is the classic cork in the organization. Of course he is blinded by his own needs. Even his name means "to nourish both together." He as the leader is attempting to nourish others but nourish himself also through the process. Doublemindedness. He is operating out of his own needs, rather than obtaining fulfillment from the Lord, then modeling Christ's sufficiency by ministering to other's needs from a loving and filled heart. Being so overly concerned with his own agenda, he cannot understand God's working even when he is sitting smack in the center of the church.

If you are secure in Christ ... you do not have to give any more structure to a situation by means of personal control than what is appropriate. Settle the issue once and for all by allowing Christ and his grace to be sufficient for your every need. Once this is accomplished, the opposite behaviors of a Diatrephes can be expected. Erase the sin of doubt and give the control to the Lord!

This will in no manner be passive ... but action-oriented faith. There ensue quite a few if-then propositions which impact self-image, self-esteem, and motivation as you grasp the emerging understanding that not only are you a child of God, but what God is doing in each believer's life is significant. There comes an anticipation for what is going to happen as God's plan for you in His kingdom begins to unfold as you "work out your salvation" in the contemporary world.

THE ONLY BASIS FOR DIVISION

The only genuine reason for division within the Christian community is the basic principle set forth in the scriptures which gives indication that there already **is** division, namely; there is no fellowship with darkness for the children of light. There is no relationship in Christ with a person who is not a part of the body of Christ. People who do not acknowledge the Lordship of Christ are not fellow members of the body ... they do not have the same basis for relationship. They are not members "one of another." They are not brothers. They are not sisters.

The Bible is quite clear about what it takes to be saved. Primarily, it is a call upon God to forgive us individually for our sin and rebellion against God, for our moral and spiritual affront to the Almighty, and our receiving by faith the free and gracious gift of salvation offered through the substitutionary death of Jesus Christ two thousand years ago. Once appropriated, the new believer experiences a relationship with God, and is born again spiritually, beginning a profound sense of belonging to God as His child, and to His family. Just like his natural family, the spiritual person has nothing to do about choosing who his other siblings may be. They are givens. And they are family, other members of the body who are to be loved, appreciated, nourished, valued and prized ... if only because of their inherent value in Christ!

For those who have come to know Jesus in a personal relationship there is no division. They are all members of the body of Christ. For those who have not repented and come to Him, there is no spiritual relationship. These already ARE divided. This is the only basis for division as the Bible puts it, the reason simply indicated is that for these two groups there IS division. Jesus likened the two groups to sheep and goats; wheat and tares; believing and unbelieving; darkness and light; just and unjust; forgiven and unforgiven; repentant and unrepentant; wise and foolish.

This alone affords the basis of separating people and in consistent Biblical fashion, people are divided from one another on the basis of their own chosen behavior. They are not to be "thinned out" by others, by leaders whose singular style or personal leadership sins force cleavage within the body of Christ.

JAMES' RATIONALE FOR CONFLICT

James, in his letter addresses this issue when he asks,

> *What causes fights and quarrels among you? Don't they come from your desires that battle within you? You want something but don't get it. You kill and covet, but you cannot have what you want. You quarrel and fight. You do not have, because you do not ask God. When you ask, you do not receive, because you ask with wrong motives, that you may spend what you get on your pleasures."* (James 4:1-3)

James is setting forth some principles of personal and group interrelationships that are at once simple and profound. He says that conflict occurs when individuals want something so much that they leave God out of the equation. That is a functional definition of covetousness. The Bible also says that God gives us "all things to enjoy," so the problem lies not in our enjoyment, but in the attempt to enjoy something aside and apart from God. Here is a subtle form of idolatry: man the god-player again.

James cites the willingness to kill with the coveting, and this bears some examination and application. As a general rule, most Christians in the church and Christian parachurch organizations do not indulge in the act of killing and/or murder today of one another. So what is James talking about?

In corporate America, an all too common experience for conflict resolution is found in power plays in which there are winners and losers. Frequently, the losers are fired and the winners go on the make their executive decisions and acquire the spoils of winning the battle. Typically, the losers carry a grudge which arises in the next confrontation, feeling that they have been bettered once, but the conflict has not been ameliorated, merely a battle has been won. Common business practice. Unfortunately, the "corporate America" syndrome can infest the thinking, values, and operating procedures of the body of Christ to the extent that leaders make similar decisions regarding those in which they find themselves in conflict, and they do all that they can to "remove" the person from the relationship. This is another form of killing someone. Unfortunately, the Roman Catholic church has had a formidable history of excommunicating those who disagreed with it in many times and cultures past.

The results are more than symbolic. Ostracism, the practice of banishment or exclusion from a group, wherein a person is shunned and rejected, can truly bring upon death. It is a severe form of denial of the person. It is nothing that was ever practiced by the Lord Jesus. It is one thing for a rich and young ruler to make the choice to walk away from the living Lord, choosing to become a counseling failure, but it is another thing for someone to send him away. Jesus always will stand at the door and knock, inviting relationship. He doesn't turn his back on anyone, much less cast one out. How can **we** justify such behavior?

James also points out that another reason for not attaining fulfillment stems from wrong motives. Isn't it marvelous that the Bible clearly indicates that some things are right and that some things are wrong! Motives can be wrong. Very wrong. Not merely unhealthy, unseemly, unattractive, offensive, or disliked. They can be *WRONG*! But James goes on to explain what may be wrong with motives ... "that you may spend what you get on your pleasures." But what does this mean?

Victor Frankl has suggested the principle that whenever a person's sense of worth and accomplishment is blunted or frustrated, he will either deflect toward power or toward pleasure to find fulfillment.

We have seen how the sin of doubt can lead a person to want control of situations and other people to a fault, building the Diatrephes power-broker syndrome. Just like the sins of power, the sins of pleasure have the same root in unbelief. The New Testament paradigm is that God has revealed Himself to us in the person of His Son, and that believing in Him gives life and meaning. The author of Hebrews wrote that "without faith it is impossible to please him." That same quality of "saving faith" is necessary for sustaining a person in terms of maintaining God-pleasing behaviors.

God created the human species with all of the pleasure reactions built in. He didn't provide such dimensionality as a lark or whim for our future frustration. This is not to suggest that mankind is incapable of debauching all of the fine gifts that God has given.

The sins of pleasure stem largely from the lack of realizing who we are as believers. When an individual recognizes that he truly is a child of the King, an ambassador for Christ, then he will have little use for indulging in the pleasures of the flesh. He will be operating on a different level. Of course the accuser will attempt to undermine that position of faith by creating doubts, influencing the believer to justify behaviors and indulge in favorite sins from the old life. But the root problem is a lack of faith.

Perhaps a better word is "trust." When we trust another we grant control to that person. It has to be a daily affair with the Lord wherein we throw the switch of our will over to His control each moment of each day. By doing this we retain meaning and purpose in every thought and action, trusting that God is at work in our human activities. We do not "miss the mark" and become diverted from our Christlike fulfillment and surrender to the temptations of power or pleasure.

In the letter from James, other therapeutic principles follow regarding the handling of conflict. To cite all of them is beyond the scope of this study, but it is noteworthy that he identifies "doublemindedness"

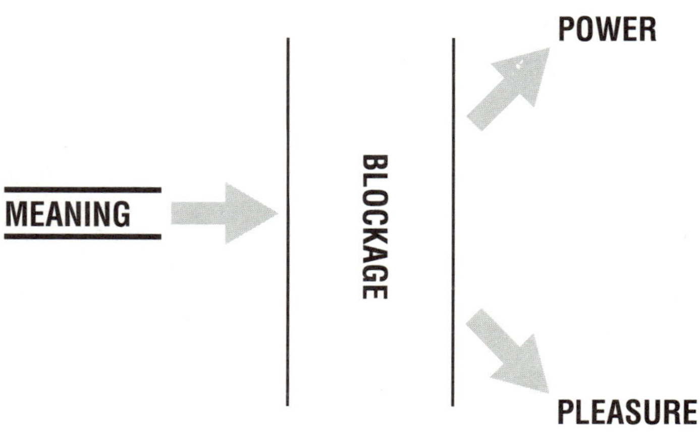

as a specific source of spiritual conflict. It holds importance not only because its effects are so obvious, but also because in everyday circumstances its occurrence is so common. Contemporary Christians must always ask, "Does this choice or behavior benefit the Lord? or is it just for me?" Again, if the believer does not settle basic issues in his walk with the Lord, remaining spiritually insecure and stunted, then he will be forever attempting to make up for something that he perceives is lacking, and that will impact both his attitudes and relationships.

Small wonder that James' admonishment is to "Submit yourselves to God." "Humble yourselves before the Lord." The primary principle is that a believer-leader has to first get the log out of his own eye before he can attempt to extricate the speck of dust that is in someone else's eye. And just as Peter had to endure the loving probe of Jesus' question about the truth of his love, so must a leader resolve his loyalty and affection regarding the Lord before he is qualified to accept any sort of commission.

In terms of leadership, because rank carries with it an enormous assemblage of privileges, there are so many perks that there is a monstrous temptation to worship and serve the office rather than the Creator. This represents the most common, though subtle, stumbling block for many contemporary leaders. Authentic contemporary leaders must examine their motives, values, and affections continuously to determine that their exercise of office is one of love and service to the Lord, and to His people. If this work of grace is left unattended or unaccomplished, then conflict, alienation and division are certain to ensue.

* * * * *

Caesar's crossing of the Rubicon, a small river in northern Italy in 49 B.C., constituted an illegal entry into Italy and thereby initiated a civil war. This basic principle, dying to self-life and the selfish preoccupation with one's own portage through life, represents a personal Rubicon for many aspiring leaders and is fraught with personal conflict; the inner civil war. For those who grow on to maturity, this concern has been effectively replaced in an assured life of the Holy Spirit's control, and is personified by the individual's ability to love freely and without recourse all people, but in a very special way, those who also know the Lord.

Notes

1. Menninger, Karl. *Whatever Became of Sin?* New York: Hawthorne Books, Inc., 1975. p. 15.
2. Ibid., p. 19.
3. Barclay, William. *A New Testament Wordbook.* New York: Harper and Brothers, 1957, p. 48.

DREAM MACHINES: BROKEN AND OTHERWISE

My daughter and her cousin Tracy were only eleven at the time. It was summer and we were living in a golf course community on the California desert, and the day dawned with the two girls and the neighbors' boys from just next door with "nothing to do." They lamented that they were sick of playing Marco Polo in the swimming pool, a rendition of hide and seek, and were pretty much bored with everything. They confronted me with their problem, seeking input.

I suggested that they write out a "wish list" of things they would like to do in life, things that they would like to experience, places they would like to go, things they would want to do. I told them not to think about how these could happen, how much they might cost, or any other problems associated with their ideas. The two girls immediately jumped on the idea, thought that it would be fun to do, and started writing their ideas out on a writing pad. The boys, a year and two years older, wouldn't touch the notion, dismissing it with the reasoning that they wouldn't be able to do anything about it anyway, so they might as well not bother to "wish."

After a little while the girls brought me their list, and I found some of their ideas well within the range of possibility requiring only a little financial development. One "wish" was a day trip to San Diego and a visit to the fabulous San Diego Zoo and Wild Animal Park. I could easily provide transportation, commuting as I was to USIU in San Diego for my doctoral studies. Knowing that they would "own" their wishes more deeply if they came with an attending vested interest, I suggested that they could earn some money if they wrote up their intended ideas on a flier and offered their services as "helpers" and "doers of odd jobs" in the surrounding neighborhood.

Finding a sympathetic neighborhood, the girls raked out an old flowerbed for one neighbor, carried out enormous stacks of newspapers for another, and concluded their entrepreneurial efforts with a cookie sale which brought in the funds for their daytrip budget.

It was a fun time. And did they ever rub it in to the two boys when they returned. Tracy reflected with a confidential aside to me, "I didn't realize that you could do whatever you want to do!" The two boys just scrunched down further where they sat, their dream machines seemingly broken beyond repair.

CHAPTER NINE

Introduction to the System Approach Contract (SAC)

Jesus asked, "Who then is the faithful and wise servant, whom his master has set over his household, to give them their food at the proper time? Blessed is that servant whom his master when he comes will find so doing." (Matt. 24:45ff)

THE SYSTEM APPROACH CONTRACT; POLYTROPHIC TOOL WITHOUT PEER!

It is fundamentally necessary for the aspiring Polytrophic leader to become equipped with tools necessary for carrying out leadership tasks that are at once effective and still inherently loving in their application. The SAC (System Approach Contract) fulfills these requirements apparently as no other leadership tool does when skillfully handled by the Polytroph. Like any other skill, learning to use the SAC takes time, commitment, effort and patience. But the benefits are significant. Let's examine a partial list of benefits.

1. The SAC is a UNIVERSAL tool. It can be used to get a handle on any kind of situation, event, movement, environment, happening or

problem. It structures thinking so that difficult situations can be effectively understood and managed.

2. The SAC is a magnificent MARKETING TOOL. Its use can provide an orderly, step-by-step representation of ideas in such a manner that it captures an audience, spurs them to action, and begets appropriate results.

3. The SAC has many LEVELS OF APPLICATION. It can be used in an Individual situation; it can be a tool for Counseling another person; it is effective in a Group setting; it can be applied to Organizations; and certainly Societies and Cultures can be examined with the SAC.

4. The SAC can be used as a MANAGEMENT DEVELOPMENT tool. Used in group and organizational development, the skilled Polytroph can delegate proper amounts of authority to group members in such a manner that people understand precisely what their level of responsibility is, what is expected of them, and when their tasks should be accomplished. There are varieties of choices available for arriving at such decisions that allow for, and depend on, the contributions of each member.

5. The SAC is a CONFLICT RESOLUTION tool. In its application, the very nature of the SAC is to identify divergent views, values, paradigms, and belief systems in an open and non-threatening manner, and then deal with the differences openly.

6. The SAC unearths HIDDEN AGENDA. It identifies divergent viewpoints in a way that draws out hidden agenda, and helps individuals evaluate their perspectives and contributions in terms of the overarching values of the problem, opportunity, or project.

7. The SAC UNSTICKS problems, people, and organizations. It demands a fresh look at problems that may have become stuck in terms of shopworn viewpoints that are ineffective in comprehending the nature of the problem or situation.

8. The SAC is an effective DIAGNOSTIC tool. It enables leaders to determine the nature of a situation or problem. It helps define the essence of what a present situation is, and forces thinking about what the situation should become.

9. The SAC MOTIVATES people so that they begin to trust God and move forward concerning any situation or problem.

10. The SAC UNITES people in a common purpose. It gathers from a diversity of opinions and perspectives, and unites groups to a commonality of understanding so that coordinated efforts can be implemented to solve problems.

11. The SAC breeds Esprit de Corps in groups. By systematically mobilizing groups to solve their internal and external problems it unites group members in a spirit of cooperation and accomplishment, providing a spirit of devotion and enthusiasm for one another, their group, and its purposes.

12. The SAC is a supreme COMMUNICATION tool. Its use offers an understanding of the scope of a situation, an appropriate definition of its parameters, an analysis of potential outcomes, alternatives, management appraisals, rationale for decision-making, and implementation strategies. It can provide a summary of complex situations in a conveniently handled arrangement.

13. The SAC is a magnificent MANAGEMENT tool. It can control the implementation of a complex solution to a complex problem. It will provide necessary information in terms that are at once understood by all involved, and sets forth the delegated tasks for all to complete. It will even provide job descriptions effectively.

14. The SAC is a FLEXIBLE tool. It can be revised as required in its implementation. It does not strangle people, groups and organizations, but frees them to organize at an appropriate level for getting things accomplished.

15. The SAC is a PLANNING tool. It is ethical to plan. Good planning can identify many alternative actions before they are to be implemented without the inherent dangers that seat-of-the-pants decision-makers instill. Proper planning removes crisis management techniques than can be so harmful to persons and organizations.

16. The SAC is an excellent illustration of wholesome SALES PSYCHOLOGY. It leads people inexorably to making decisions, answering the basic question, "Why should I select this alternative from among all possible alternatives?"

17. The SAC evidences PROFESSIONALISM. Handled properly, it answers all questions of how and why an individual, group or organization does what it does. It demonstrates the virtue of solid preparation, of "doing one's homework."

18. The SAC WORKS. It does get the task accomplished ... and it does grow people ... and groups ... and organizations!

THE SAC AS POLYTROPHIC TOOL; THE SEVEN STEPS

The SAC is an orderly, seven step technique for Polytrophic leaders to use in the formulation of significant tasks for individuals, small groups, and organizations.

Step One represents a Needs Assessment, the depiction of difference between "What Is" (WI) and "What Should Be" (WSB), and is the most important exercise in determining authentic needs. It necessarily plumb-bobs value systems, paradigms, milieu, organizational cultures, leadership styles, and descriptive language in groups and organizations.

Step Two is a process for determining what outcomes the group wants to accomplish regarding the needs they have identified. An outcome is a measurable statement which tells what, where, who, how many, when, what kind, under which circumstances, etc. It is a quantifiable summation of WHAT SHOULD BE statements. This step also becomes a means of accountability, for it represents a measurable method of monitoring group processes. This SAC benefit stands in stark contrast to vicarious ministries wherein someone else represents the funder, and seeks to accomplish ministry "on-behalf-of" the supporter, usually with no accountability feedback loops other than casual newsletters.

Step Three, a process of identifying alternatives, demands the courage to create. Combining thorough attention to exhausting all possibilities of going from WI to WSB, it draws upon the groups resources to think through and create imaginative methods and means of getting the job done. This step includes an evaluation of advantages and disadvantages of each alternative solution which is identified. Effectively accomplished, this step in the SAC process will generate fresh ideas without the constraints of habitual norms, rigid stereotypical thinking, bias or prejudice.

Step Four is critical decision-making based on the information of Step Three, where if adequate and conclusive work is accomplished, these decisions should be obvious. As a built-in to the problem solving methodology, the SAC forces leader groups to a point of commitment, thereby unfreezing situations, and providing movement toward predetermined goals.

Step Five acknowledges the realization that the best of decisions remains ineffective if not adequately implemented. The skilled Polytrophic leader becomes a manager at this point in the process, using basic controlling tools such as PERT-charts, function-flow diagrams, and disbursing operational levels of authority to carry out tasks. Suitable reporting and feedback loops are created, as well as the scheduling of accomplishments.

Step Six requires the measurement of results, indicating if the needs have been met or not met. The group will review the intent of Step Two and determine if they have changed the situation to "What Should Be." Understood as a method of accountability rather than as a function of judgmental condemnation, this step urges the identification of changing equations, the investigation of fresh problems, and the assessment of additional needs.

Step Seven actually functions throughout the entire SAC process rather than following a linear progression. Step Seven states "Revise as Required." In normal applications of the SAC, many forces may impact the situation which the leadergroup is undertaking to change, making necessary revisions in the process as it is being implemented. When this occurs, the leadergroup must make appropriate changes and reapply the SAC process from that step forward. Handled in this fashion, The SAC represents a pliable tool for flexible, caring leaders.

A PLANNING TOOL

The SAC must ultimately be considered as a planning tool, and Polytrophic leaders recognize that it is ethical to plan. Just as a banquet is planned with proper seating for the guests; table decorations selected, created and in place; the food meticulously and industriously prepared, skillfully presented on serving platters, and graciously offered by attentive waiters, so too are Polytrophic leaders to be adept at the planning process.

Most importantly, it is highly ethical to plan. Skillful planners can examine a variety of scenarios "on paper" before they are implemented, and by so doing they eliminate the dangerous results of those whose seat-of-the-pants decision making creates the kinds of adverse situations wherein others can get hurt. With proper planning, alternatives can be scrutinized, their advantages and disadvantages evaluated before any individual is at risk.

In contrast, the typical power-broker controller fights to limit access to the planning process. Of the glaring faults indicative of the authoritarian person, his penchant for committing human and other resources on whim without the rigorous sifting by multiple minds, habitually creates situations injurious to those who may attempt to carry out such tasks. For those who have been "had" through such encounters, there is a deep appreciation for a healthy planning process and the attending contributions that circumspect persons can make when there is access to the planning table.

ON MISSION

Churches and Christian organizations should know what their mission is all about, i.e., what are their distinctives? What is their market? Is it just some vague disposition to preach the gospel? To whom? On what basis? Usually the "gospel preaching" is done to the membership to keep them satisfied with the preacher, and reinforce group values. While these experiences may be comforting to those who polish pews every Sunday, it has little to do with fulfilling the Great Commission.

OF LOVE

A church or Christian organization must accomplish a needs assessment so that they can respond to those needs IN LOVE. It is the ability to respond to needs that sets off the obedient, diligent, vital, contemporary church from those who "talk a good game," but merely go through the motions. Akin to the "good Samaritan," the needs-oriented group is the one that is operating IN LOVE, and thereby fulfilling the great commandments of the Lord. Anything else is self-deception, compromise and spiritually dead.

Paul was adamant about not building on someone else's foundation. He wanted to go where the needs were the greatest. He saw no purpose in going to a group where there was already someone operating to meet needs. In our contemporary church scene there are groups stumbling constantly over one another in competitive attempts to garner the Christian donors' dollar in order to justify their existence. But they are not focusing on meeting the horrific needs that exist in contemporary society in terms of social, economic, and human needs—all of which are ultimately spiritual needs.

HISTORICAL BURDEN OF GOD'S PEOPLE

Believers of each age hold the responsibility of reiterating the historical, life-changing truths of the Gospel of Jesus Christ to their generation, preparing others to likewise be equipped for their succeeding generations. It seems obvious that the contemporary church has failed on a large scale to accomplish this.

Currently, secular humanism has risen to the rank of popular religion for modern education. Increased scientific technology has outstripped considerations of ethics to the extent that if a technique or scientific "breakthrough" is achieved, there appears to be small consideration of whether or not such techniques should be applied to the human equation. The attitude seems to be, "If we can do a thing, do it!" The ramifications of such decisions are left unconcernedly to some other group of thinkers to supposedly debate the ethics of their work. The contemporary national debate over abortion represents only one such incidence of these dynamics. Perhaps it is too much to expect that those who today create research and development of products for human application also integrate a value base which is sensitive to moral and spiritual realities.

A CALL FOR ENLIGHTENMENT

The challenge for today's Christian certainly involves understanding the impact of modern technology on traditional values, beliefs and behaviors. If not confronted and handled from an intelligent, biblical, and spiritual perspective, these unchecked technologies will continue to undermine and erode a Christian basis for choices and behaviors, if only from their sheer mesmerizing alternatives. It does not have to work this way, but if there is no enlightened counterbalancing of Godless notions, the contemporary church will always be defensive, trying to catch up with a rampant technology which steamrolls sacred principles, those that edify and promote decency, uplift the human spirit, and reinforces that personal relationship with God. Rightfully handled, technology in the hands of caring, sensitive, polytrophic leaders can be a continued force for alleviating human suffering, injustice, and spiritual bondage. Considering how the church has historically dragged behind in its classical illustration of cultural lag, it is not too hard to build a case for the necessity of contemporary Christians to stop their intellectual wool-gathering, their fraternal spats, their head-in-the-sand posture, and confront a godless world with the full blown gospel.

Not incidentally, this is a Gospel that has the capacity to gather and unite all of the world's issues and concerns in a concerted effort of timely understanding. The biblical paradigms still are the basis of truth. Our loving God is still a righteous God. He IS the great creator. We DO live in the middle of spiritual warfare. We DO have significant human limitations; "we see darkly." God DOES have a purpose and plan which He is working out through history. Through Jesus we can not only know Him, but become involved in His eternal activities. If these truths are communicated effectively, then responses to identified needs in the form of insightful therapies can become commonplace practice among those who are authentic believers. Is anything as unassailable as agape love in action?

CHANGE

It has been repeated frequently that, in view of the increased pace of change, we must prepare to cope with change. Many contemporary leaders suggest that change is the only thing that we can be sure of today. If they are correct, their analysis offers only more rationale for increased awareness, increased capacities and skills to respond to an ever changing world by those flexible leaders who can discriminate between good and evil, and do the fitting thing at the appropriate time.

Change allows for the development of creative new ways of looking at things—new paradigms, fresh observations in light of contemporary trends. The appropriate and skilled use of the SAC can generate an infinite array of responses to identified needs, providing vital glimpses of timeless truths. But it is imperative that contemporary Christians understand the raw gospel Jesus offered in the context of the first century. Given this insight, the doors of opportunity stand ajar for today's believers to create mighty deeds of testimony and achievement that will forever bear their rewards.

GROWTH THROUGH INVOLVEMENT

While it must be acknowledged that the church does have a responsibility of meeting the needs of its members, I suggest that the better way is to grow members by involving them in the work of the Lord through the local church and its mission. Too frequently there exists the notion on the part of church leaders that a person has to acquire some level of perfection, quite a few steps beyond simple competency, before they are allowed to exercise any gifts or function in the body. While the teachings of the Apostles and church fathers are quick to assert that no novices take on responsibilities for which they have no depth to perform adequately, there are numerous opportunities for growing persons to contribute significantly through the local church body if appropriately "mentored" or guided by more mature people. This function of guiding must also include the growth of their attitudes, reasoning, and evaluating skills; the "renewing of their minds" (Rom. 12:1-2.) kinds of input, keeping in mind that these followers are being groomed for positions of considerable leadership roles wherever the Lord may place them in the future.

This is, after all, how the Lord developed his disciples. There were some hard lessons to be learned. Remember the account in the gospels of the Lord Jesus telling the disciples to get into the boat and row across the lake to Bethsaida after he fed the five thousand? (See Matt. 14:23ff, Mk. 6:45ff and Jn.6:16ff) The men were obedient, but after rowing through the night, certainly at the point of exhaustion, they became fearful. Of course the Lord knew that people are more susceptible to suggestion when they are spent physically. Mark says they were terrified when Jesus came to them, walking on the water, but notes, *"they did not understand about the loaves, but their hearts were hardened."* Would the Lord use the terrors of our imaginations to teach us a hard lesson? Read the accounts!

But as we attempt to emulate the Lord's training and discipling will there be mistrakes? (sic) As surely as a plebian pianist may ping off key! Both leaders and learners can miss the mark. Those instances may very well happen. But they should not be the norm, given proper supervision and preparation. And if the leadergroup constantly reinforces an overarching environment of growth and preparation as its focus within the group, there will be greater understanding of these occasional errors. It will not adversely affect worship or functionality when understood in this context.

SENSITIVITIES

As Polytrophic leaders learn to apply the SAC, they will of necessity be models of love in action, fortifying afresh a sense of the worth and dignity of each person involved with the process. At each step of the procedure he will be certain to elicit feedback and consensus within the group by asking such typical questions as, "Does anyone feel uncomfortable with this decision?" "Are there other concerns that have not been addressed here?" "Do we, as a group, have peace about this decision?" "Have we examined all alternatives?"

When the SAC is handled effectively, group members will sense a great level of trust so that they can feel free to explore, free to fail, and free to create.

LATERAL THINKING

Many years ago when a person who owed money could be thrown into jail, a merchant in London had the misfortune to owe a huge sum to a money-lender. The money-lender, who was old and ugly, fancied the merchant's beautiful teenage daughter. He proposed a bargain. He said he would cancel the merchant's debt if he could have the girl instead.

Both the merchant and his daughter were horrified at the proposal. So the cunning money-lender proposed that they let Providence decide the matter. He told them that he would put a black pebble and a white pebble into an empty money-bag and then the girl would have to pick out one of the pebbles. If she chose the black pebble she would become his wife and her father's debt would be cancelled. If she chose the white pebble she would stay with her father and the debt would still be cancelled. But if she refused to pick out a pebble her father would be thrown into jail and she would starve.

Reluctantly the merchant agreed. They were standing on a pebble-strewn path in the merchant's garden as they talked and the money-lender stooped down to pick up the two pebbles. As he picked up the two pebbles the girl, sharp eyed with fright, noticed that he picked up two black pebbles and put them into the money-bag. He then asked the girl to pick out the pebble that was to decide her fate and that of her father.

Imagine that you are standing on that path in the merchant's garden. What would you have done if you were that unfortunate girl? If you had to advise her what would you advise her to do? What type of thinking would you use to solve the problem?

The girl in the pebble story put her hand into the money-bag and drew out a pebble. Without looking at it she fumbled and let it fall to the path where it was immediately lost among all the others.

"Oh, how clumsy of me" she said, "but never mind— if you look into the bag you will be able to tell which pebble I took by the color of the one that is left." —Edward De Bono, in *New Think* (Avon Books, 1968)

CHAPTER TEN

SAC Polytrophic Tool Without Peer

The SAC is an orderly, seven step technique for Polytrophic leaders to use in the formulation of significant tasks for individuals, small groups, and organizations which structures and organizes them for predetermined results in keeping with Biblical values of love, and the worth and dignity of those with whom he works.

So where does a group begin?

At the beginning! Let us work through the various steps of the SAC, discussing the reasoning for each and every step identified, indicating how best to work the system. (For your personal worksheet use space enough to allow extensive notes and remarks.)

SAC: SYSTEM APPROACH CONTRACT WORKSHEET
(Outline)

Magnitude of Application Levels:

1. Individual
2. Counseling
3. Group
4. Organizational
5. Societal

I. Needs Assessment:

A need is the measurable gap between "What Is" and "What Should Be."

WHAT IS	WHAT SHOULD BE
1.	1.
2.	2.
3.	3.
4.	4.

II. Determine Outcomes:

An outcome is a measurable statement which tells what, where, who, how many, when, what kind, under which circumstances, etc. It is a quantifiable summation of WHAT SHOULD BE statements.

III. Identify Alternatives:

This is an appropriately exhaustive rendering of all the possible ways of going from WHAT IS to WHAT SHOULD BE. It also includes identifying the advantages and disadvantages of each:

	Alternative Solution	Advantages/Disadvantages
1.		
2.		
3.		
4.		
5.		
6.		

IV. Select Alternative(s):

The Decision-maker based on step III above. If step III is fully developed, this decision will probably be obvious.

V. Implement Alternative:

Implementation strategy includes the identification of what activities will be accomplished, by whom, with what authority, and a scheduled date of accomplishment; ideally it will display a function-flow diagram/PERT chart.

VI. Measure Results:

Review Step II above: Need met or not met. Has equation changed? Is new needs assessment recommended?

VII. Revise as Required:

At any point in the implementation of the SAC forces may impact the equation which may require revision. Make appropriate changes and reapply the SAC from that Point.

STEP ONE: NEEDS ASSESSMENT

A need can be defined as the measurable difference between "what is" and "what should be." Generally speaking, it is usually not too difficult to obtain base line data on "what is," the present state of affairs, what is going on in a given situation, relationship, group, organization or culture. Questionnaires can be structured to elicit responses, tests can be adapted to the environment under consideration, even standardized testing can be readily effective in providing the necessary information to determine where a situation really is. One technique that I have used very effectively is the use of a structured interview of individuals who make up a corporate population and culture. It is a somewhat time-consuming process, but seemingly without peer in developing rapport and trust with groups with which there is anticipated intervention and change.

Determining "what should be" can become a difficult task, primarily because most organizations hold within them all sorts of hidden agenda. Different people have differing ideas about where a group "should be." Also, because of differing building blocks of personality, different people see things differently; they create different paradigms of reality when observing the same or similar situations. Their experiences, emotional states, values, impressions, and sensitivities all can impact individual perceptions. It is a wonder that any two people can really agree on anything!

A necessary step in gathering data for a needs assessment therefore requires a certain level of communication and conflict resolution skills by those who assume the role of facilitator. Frequently, group norms dictate how conflicts are handled. If, for example, the group normally operates with a "power mode," where might makes right, conflicts are usually determined on a win-lose basis. Whoever has the authority in a given circumstance rules the day. Unfortunately, those who lose many times live to fight again another day, and they bring with them into the next conflict the aggrieved attitudes resultant from past encounters. Ultimately, many may choose to withdraw.

"What should be" also includes a sweep of values inherent in any group. Normal diversity of perspectives, experience, value-programming, and personality differentiation will provide a wide range of responses to "what should be." It takes considerable time and effort to sort through these alternatives and arrive at a consensus for the organization in such a way that the consensus is not forced or contrived.

Of course, it is always quite simple to take input from the highest echelon of leadership and attempt to adopt that as the "what should be" statement, but that tends to beg the question, that is, it will not be an authentic reflection of those who make up the culture. Eventually any further activity based on such a need statement will necessarily be skewed in the direction of the power elite, and probably not obtain the desired ends for the group.

A thorough and proper use of a Needs Assessment by a group can gather and unite the group by skillfully unearthing hidden agenda in a non-threatening way. The facilitator must communicate by words, attitude and actions that all perceptions of What Is (WI) and What Should Be (WSB) are legitimate if sincerely held, credibly supported, and borne out by underlying data. Depending on the maturity of members in the group, and the cohesiveness of the group, it may be necessary for the Polytrophic Leader to draw out divergent opinions, seeking to bring forth possibly obvious, or threatening considerations which the group may not have been willing to examine before without the process of the SAC as a motivating force to do so. Skillfully and sensitively probed, the Needs Assessment can become a breath of the fresh air of renewal for many groups.

The Needs Assessment is the messiest step of the SAC because it initially seems to provide less structure than a group may sense is workable. With practice, however, group members and individuals begin to learn about appropriate levels of abstraction, begin to think on similar levels, and to deal effectively with their individual differences in a supportive fashion once they recognize the benefits of diversity. During this "messy" period, facilitators can readily expect those who have control needs will attempt to impose their will on the process. If they are successful in captivating everyone involved, they will attempt to shut down the process, fearful of not being able to control each person and every idea. When this occurs, a facilitator has to identify the conduct openly for the group, advising the group of the consequences of such behavior, and allowing the group to censor the offending party so as to continue the process.

One of the most powerful uses of the Needs Assessment can be the development of short statements or sentences which clearly depict an aspect of WHAT IS, then in linear juxtaposition write out the corollary WHAT SHOULD BE statement. By so doing, the statements build up a "trip-hammer" effect which can powerfully represent an "unfreezing" strategy, so that the group begins to realize that something must be done, the status quo will no longer suffice.

NEEDS ARE "MEASURABLE" GAPS BETWEEN WI AND WSB

Depending on the sophistication and overall depth of the sense of stewardship which the group holds, the process is greatly enhanced by defining as distinctly as possible the measurable difference between WI and WSB. A need, after all, is defined as "the measurable difference between WI and WSB." The measures selected will become the milepost of feedback as the group begins movement towards WSB. In this context, arbitrary decisions about the timing of certain outcomes expected by the group can be made, depending on events or concerns which may impact such decisions. All of the seven steps above should be further qualified with the attending phrase "as measured by"... and then display the selected measuring instruments that tell when, where, how many, at what time, under what circumstances, etc. Perceived or "felt" needs may not pass scrutiny when compared to needs that stand up to examination based on hard data. Again, when initiating the SAC with groups who are not normally used to operating in a systematic manner, these considerations represent the "fine-tuning" of the instrument.

For those who are comfortable with the discipline of planning their work and working their plan, the creation of measurements represents an important predetermination of acceptable outcomes. For example, let us suppose that a group believes that before God and country their small church of 100 members should grow significantly within the next fiscal year. Given input about normal church growth in an area such as theirs, they arbitrarily define that "growth" as 200 members one year hence. Such creative measuring is merely a device for getting a handle on a situation, and does not imply that God is in any sort of "theological planning box," but that the group members have come to some level of working consensus for the sake of modeling "what if" scenarios. They have a basis for selection strategies for creating workable paradigms in terms of their stewardship of church growth. In this sense, their measuring strategies reflect the group's goal-setting ambitions, which when straight-forwardly published by the group can become a legitimate motivational technique for assigning tasks within the group. Like all skills acquisitions, learning better ways to measure situations will grow with the necessity of doing so.

Notice that the Needs Assessment statements in the following illustration do not lack value judgements, but represent consensus statements of those who were involved in the planning and documentation process for that ministry. Because of the anticipated application of the SAC in their specific ministry, there was collaboration and consensus that additional detail was not needed at that time. The process served extremely well at such a level and communicated the nature of the ministry and how it was to be implemented, based on the succeeding steps of the SAC.

A group of Christian golfers decided to explore the possibility of a ministry using, Moses-like, the "staff" which was in their hands, only this group's "staffs" were drivers, woods, irons, and putters. They wanted to reach other golfers for Christ and were attempting to think through a justifiable framework and strategy for doing so. They called themselves "The Masters' Golf Tour" and created the following Needs Assessment. Notice that such a listing communicates very simply a need ... a gap, between where things are and where they should be. This information, so structured, provided the basis for all subsequent choices, behaviors, and actions.

WHAT IS.	WHAT SHOULD BE
1. Little opportunity for Christian golfers to exercise their ability for the glory of God.	1. A viable option for Christian golfers to use their golfing ability to the glory of God.
2. Christians who play golf may see the game as an obstruction to their more important responsibilities.	2. Christian golfers given opportunity to use their golfing interests in a constructive way for spiritual enrichment.
3. Little opportunity for Christians to have "fellowship" across church denominational lines.	3. Christians given opportunity to share commonality of experience in non-proselytizing atmosphere.
4. Limited perspective of churches to use all means available to them for outreach and evangelism.	4. A model of the use of special interest which gives benefit to the entire body of Christ in terms of outreach and evangelism.
5. Limited opportunity for layman to develop skills, knowledge, and ability in outreach and evangelism.	5. Opportunity provided for laymen to develop skills, knowledge and ability in leadership.
6. Pastors have no program available which will reach the leadership community of business, educators, & government through contacts established on the commonality of interests such as golf.	6. A program, which when implemented, will establish contact with "leadership community" in many branches.
7. Golf represents an idol to some individuals; #1 in their values.	7. Golf used as a tool for influence, thereby more appropriately situated in personal scale of values.

STEP TWO: DETERMINE OUTCOMES, THE ACCOUNTABILITY MEASURE

In terms of the SAC, an outcome statement provides a description of acceptable, desirable, predetermined results which can be measured. It will describe circumstances, growth, numbers, levels of knowledge, and even people. This step essentially reflects a summary of WSB statements. It will tell what, where, who, how many, when, what kind, and under what circumstances. Here, in a sense, the leader-group selects its own yardstick to measure its future accomplishments. It is a way of asking, "How will we know when we have gone from WI to WSB?" While some results may not be as obvious as others, this step does tend to guarantee that a group or organization does not simply justify adverse results of their choices, behaviors and decisions by glibly claiming that their "real" purposes were something else. It is

> The Christian golfing group developed the following Solution Requirement:
>
> Christian golfers will have an opportunity to use golfing skills, knowledge and abilities in a manner which will influence others toward examining the claims of Christ and experiencing the Lordship of Christ as measured in the following way:
>
> 1. Each activity provided by Christian golfers will have significant numbers of participants; each event will carry itself financially; each participant will cover his own expenses.
> 2. The activities will illustrate an appropriate placement of golf in a person's value and belief system.
> 3. Activities will indicate a wise use of resources as expressed in the Word of God.
> 4. Individuals who have experienced change and growth as a result of the influence of Christian golfers in their lives will bear testimony.
> 5. Participants will become involved in discipleship programs and actively disciple others.
> 6. Evangelized participants in golfing activities will join local churches and become responsible members.

impossible to create square circles. Yet I have seen leaders get off the track of planned change, arrive elsewhere, and then give ludicrous excuses for the results they have obtained. Accountability still represents value to the wise steward!

STEP THREE: IDENTIFY ALTERNATIVES, Courageous Creativity

An organization or group can have a lot of enjoyment when it arrives at this point in the SAC due to the exercise of the unique gifts from among its members. This represents the "Think Tank" phase of the SAC and the best climate is one of non-judgmental, unfettered anticipation, heavily laced with joyous humor. Sometimes an off-the-wall idea may have the germ of significant possibilities. This should not at all suggest that the exhaustive documentation of alternatives be devoid of calculated reasoning or the disciplined outworking of logical and obvious alternatives. However, if there is an opportunity to look at situations with fresh paradigms, new insights, unusual combinations of thoughts and ideas, the freedom from old stereotypes, here is the place!

Creativity is generated by many complex stimulations, not all of which are understood. Guilt can dampen the creative process, as can absorbing worries and fear. Rollo May contributes:

> We cannot will to have insights. We cannot will creativity. But we can will to give ourselves to the encounter with intensity of dedication and commitment. The deeper aspects of awareness are activated to the extent that the person is committed to the encounter.[1]

Nietzche, in his important book The Birth of Tragedy, cites the Dionysian principle of surging vitality and the Apollonian principle of form and rational order as the two dialectic principles that operate in creativity..[2] Certainly, as the Polytrophic facilitator works through the SAC, those who have greater intellectual and spiritual discipline will normally contribute more beneficially to the process than the less mature. The wise leader will also notice that the types of suggestions offered appear as a litmus test of awareness and possibly, maturity.

The Christian golfers considered the following Solution Alternatives, citing their advantages and disadvantages:

1. Develop an organization exclusively for the purpose of honoring God by the creation, scheduling, promotion, and management of golfing activities.

   Disadvantages: Takes time, effort and limited resources, and organization alone does not produce results.

   Advantages: An organizational structure is a probable and necessary subgoal to reach solution.

2. Utilize the successful outreach and evangelism strategy of banquet meetings similar to those used by the Christian Business Mens' Committee (CBMC) and the Full Gospel Business Mens' Fellowship International (FGBMFI) and combine it with a golf tournament and associated activities.

   Disadvantages: Take time, energy, and limited financial resources.

   Advantages: Would meet solution requirements.

3. Train and equip Christian golfers to share their faith wherever and whenever they play golf.

   Disadvantages: Time consuming, limited training resources presently available; such activities may be inappropriate in certain situations.

   Advantages: Would possibly meet some solution requirements.

4. Christian golfers can sponsor activities for junior golfers (up to age 18) indicating loving Christian concern.

   Disadvantages: Would reach partial golfing population directly with limited peer influence; financial, time and energy expenditures necessary.

   Advantages: It would indirectly fulfill solution requirements, spilling influence over to parents.

5. Christians can motivate golf professionals to provide appropriate golfing activities.

Disadvantages: Would provide limited personal involvement; would not necessarily meet solution requirement.
Advantages: Perhaps a lesser expenditure of resources.

6. Christian golfers can play golf shouting "Praise the Lord" after each shot instead of cursing and swearing.
   Disadvantages: Limited surface orientation to the problem.
   Advantages: Golf could be a little easier on the ears!
7. Christian golfers can produce, publish and distribute Christian oriented golfing literature and mass media productions.
   Disadvantages: Costly, time consuming; tends toward impersonal influence.
   Advantages: Could reach multiplied numbers of people interested in golf.
8. Christian golfers can do nothing, trusting that by some supernatural intervention, these opportunities will somehow be provided for them to reach the golf world.
   Disadvantages: Not too likely to happen.
   Advantages: No expenditure; no risk!

More mature individuals will carry with their creative alternatives the appreciations of both advantages and disadvantages which accompany each suggested alternative. All too frequently, as people "mature" they leave behind the childhood capacity to dream, to imagine, to create.

As each alternative is identified, a comprehensive examination of the Advantages and Disadvantages must eventually accompany the alternative. Those with expertise in a related discipline can add to the pool of knowledge by providing any missing information regarding the suggested alternative. If the group does a complete job at this point, it is relatively easy to make astute decisions as to which alternatives should be implemented.

STEP FOUR: SELECT ALTERNATIVE(S)

Decisions! Decisions! Decisions!

The SAC process parallels bonafide sales psychology at this juncture because it seeks to answer the question, "Why select this alternative above all of the other possible alternatives?" Wholesome and proper salesmanship, without manipulative ploys, will seek to bring a person or group to such a decision based on logical input, buttressed by recognizable supporting data, including benefits. If and when all other alternatives have been duly considered, the group or organization can move on to the next step.

The uncommitted sometimes are unable to make decisions because they are unwilling to make the commitment. They perceive that freedom is synonymous with the ability to change their mind whenever an easier path seems available. Sometimes they are unwilling to live with the consequences of their choices, so they procrastinate in the hope that circumstances will change and they will not have to stand up and be counted.

The SAC demands that individuals and groups throw the switch, take the plunge, bite the bullet, and ... make the decision. If authentic preparation or "homework" has been done, there can radiate a sense of group accomplishment knowing that it has galvanized for action. They have met the enemy, and for sure, it AIN'T US! There is a certain vindication for all of the preliminary work up to this point.

A comparison should be made at this step of the SAC between the Polytrophic leader and the power-brokering authoritarian type. The A type personality has done his own homework, based on his own perceptions of WI and WSB, determined the desirable outcomes from his own perspective, and selected his own set of alternatives (usually with controls benefitting himself), and seeks to persuade others by Machiavellian methods to back him in his quest for control of the process and its outcomes. Research indicates that authoritarian leaders tend to use the SAC only to reinforce their own status, power, and control, usually on relatively simple problems.[3] His mind is closed. He has chosen not to see, blinded by his own insecurities.

Polytrophs seek to draw out the wisdom of the group, nurturing their choices and processes, and discovering with the group what is best. Having no control needs, they serve the group in shepherding it to its finest hour, depending on the Lord to work through the members of the body. He is open and flexible, yet will resource the group if insights as to Biblical truths are overlooked or neglected. He will speak the truth in love, even when it hurts. He models commitment by his very commitment to love each member of the group. His strength is displayed in meekness; he does not have to be pushy.

> Our golfing group selected the following solutions from the identified alternatives: #'s 1, 2, and 3 above and summarized their choices with the following statement:
>
> Christian golfers will be given opportunities by fellow Christian golfers to constructively exercise their golfing skills, knowledge, and ability to the glory of God by the development and deployment of an evangelism program which encompasses commonly used strategies for outreach. The program will consist of golf tournaments followed by the successful format of a banquet for all participants where Christian golfers can share their personal testimony of saving faith in the person and work of Jesus Christ. This program will serve as a model of the use of special interest groups for the benefit of the body of Christ, the church, and other parachurch organizations.

STEP FIVE: IMPLEMENT ALTERNATIVE(S)

Implementation strategies include what activities will take place, in what order, by whom, with what authority, and define the scheduled date of completion. Basic management skills readily apply, but sometimes are not as obvious as they might be in Christian organizations including the church.

The issue of authority can be handled in terms of the following suggested guidelines. Leaders should be reminded that enormous frustration breeds in the lives of individuals who are tasked with responsibilities, but lack the authority to carry those tasks to completion. Responsibility without authority can break the spirit of the finest leader. The five following levels of authority, if adequately spelled out, can prevent considerable grief when implementing an alternative to reach group and its organizational goals:

Five Levels of Authority

1. "Gather data for me and I will decide."

   This level is best utilized when working with immature people or individuals with whom the leader is unfamiliar. As the highest level of control, risk is minimal to the leader. This level can also be used as a modeling tool to acquaint new followers with group and organizational practices, policies and norms. The use of this level can also become a teaching device for the benefit of less mature persons by structuring information-gathering chores in a manner in which the learner can assimilate the nature of the tasks, the basis for the schedule, and what priorities should be maintained. Again, in true Polytrophic fashion, a caring leader will be concerned for the growing awareness of his subordinates and yokefellows, and will with candor attempt to increase their awareness during the SAC process.

2. "Investigate and make recommendations to me and we will decide together."

   The second level of authority takes into consideration the value of the follower's contributions. The leader at this level is relying on the nature of the information provided, and also on the construct of what is presented to him and from which the joint decision is to be made. It is a level which permits the associate to invest his own values, paradigms, and frame of reference into the equation which reflects the co-worker's growing ability to assume responsibility.

3. "Do it and report back immediately."

   At level three the associate has the full authority to complete the task as he sees fit within predetermined parameters, but is commanded to report back immediately so that the leader can determine the consequences of the associate's activities and their overall impact on the project's forward movement. The co-worker enjoys more freedom to accomplish tasks in terms of his own style, but still has tight reins of accountability in terms of timely reporting to his leader.

4. "Do it and report back to me routinely."

   This level is most comfortably used when the associate has demonstrated his ability to complete tasks and developed an attending level of trust, understanding, and predictability. People working at this level have generally developed a cohesiveness within the group and can anticipate what others will think, say, and do.

5. "Do it and don't report back."

The ultimate level of authority in which complete control and responsibility is vested in the associate. The person has earned the right to carry out the task as he sees fit, comfortable that what he does will be done completely, correctly, and in accordance with the group's expectations. Obviously, this level of authority is reserved for mature persons who have demonstrated their proficiency in comprehending the task to be accomplished and displayed their craftsmanship through other completed work which is readily identifiable.

FUNCTION-FLOW DIAGRAMS AND PERT CHARTS

An easy tool which leaders can use to plan and monitor progress in implementing a solution alternative is the Function-Flow Diagram. In its simplest form the leader merely lists in chronological order the steps that are to be accomplished, numbers them accordingly, creates "blocks" or "boxes" for labelling each step, and then ties the labelled boxes together with "action lines" depicting the direction of the flow of steps which will be taken as the group implements the alternative.

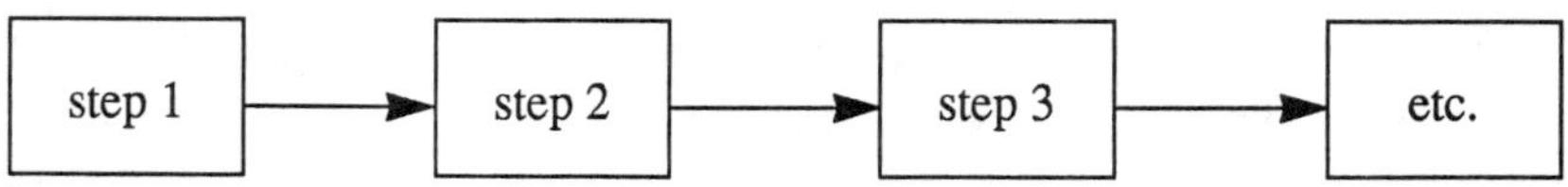

A modification of the FFD is accomplished by adding additional space to indicate both the person directly responsible for the action-step to be completed, and the date scheduled for completion. This modification begins to resemble the naval Program Evaluation and Retrieval Technique (PERT) chart.

This additional control factor allows supervision to be easily accomplished even when the leader is not present when actions are being taken. He can determine where the project is, what steps have been completed, whether work is on schedule or not, identify critical paths, and expedite corrective measures quickly.

The Christian golfers developed the following Function-Flow Diagram depicting the steps taken to implement their evangelistic golf outreach program:

(see following diagrams)

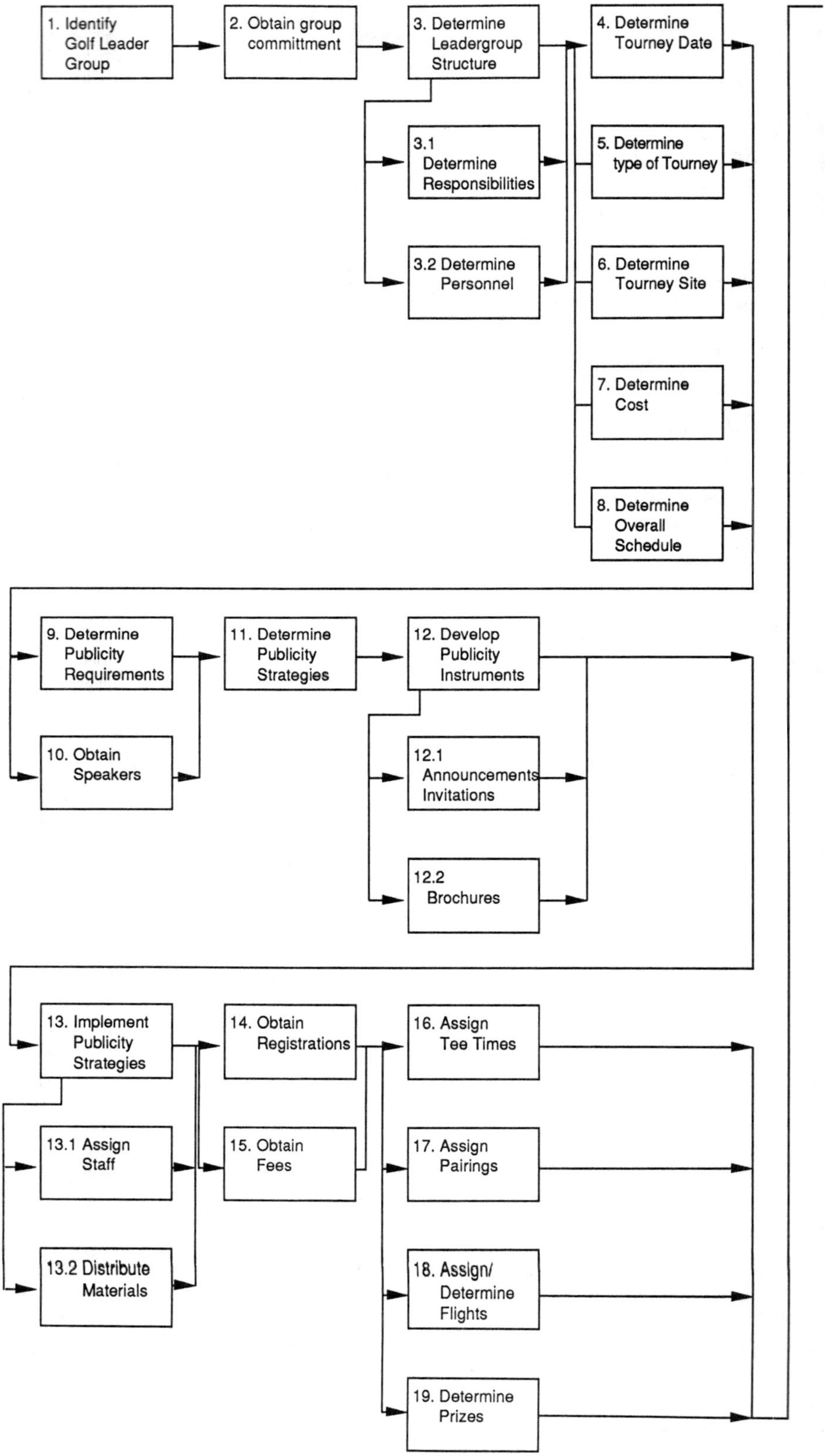

1. Identify Golf Leader Group
2. Obtain group committment
3. Determine Leadergroup Structure
3.1 Determine Responsibilities
3.2 Determine Personnel
4. Determine Tourney Date
5. Determine type of Tourney
6. Determine Tourney Site
7. Determine Cost
8. Determine Overall Schedule
9. Determine Publicity Requirements
10. Obtain Speakers
11. Determine Publicity Strategies
12. Develop Publicity Instruments
12.1 Announcements Invitations
12.2 Brochures
13. Implement Publicity Strategies
13.1 Assign Staff
13.2 Distribute Materials
14. Obtain Registrations
15. Obtain Fees
16. Assign Tee Times
17. Assign Pairings
18. Assign/ Determine Flights
19. Determine Prizes

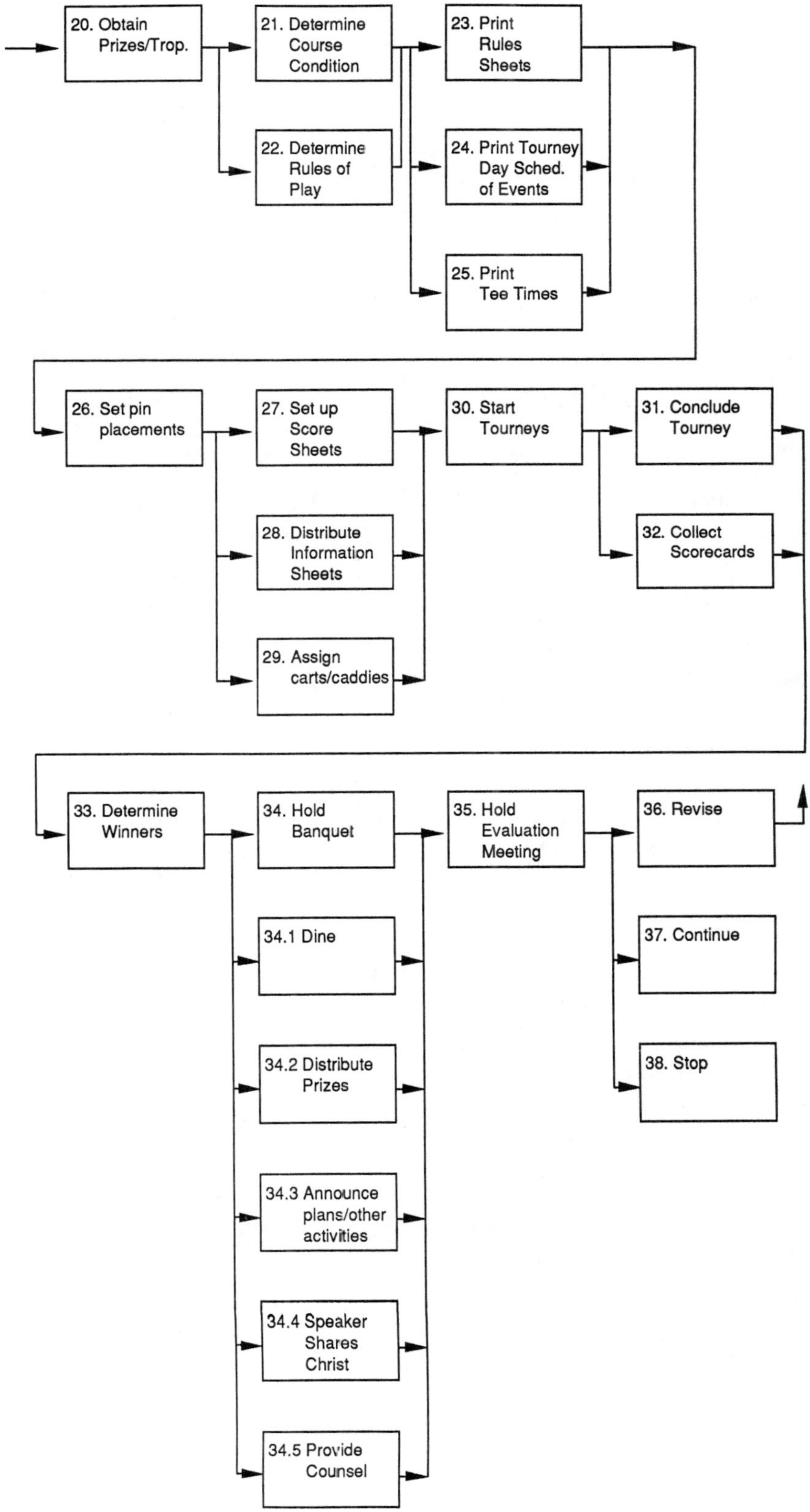
20. Obtain Prizes/Trop.
21. Determine Course Condition
22. Determine Rules of Play
23. Print Rules Sheets
24. Print Tourney Day Sched. of Events
25. Print Tee Times
26. Set pin placements
27. Set up Score Sheets
28. Distribute Information Sheets
29. Assign carts/caddies
30. Start Tourneys
31. Conclude Tourney
32. Collect Scorecards
33. Determine Winners
34. Hold Banquet
34.1 Dine
34.2 Distribute Prizes
34.3 Announce plans/other activities
34.4 Speaker Shares Christ
34.5 Provide Counsel
35. Hold Evaluation Meeting
36. Revise
37. Continue
38. Stop

STEP SIX: MEASURE RESULTS

To evaluate any project, goals must be measurable and results must be measured. The SAC certainly has many built-in qualities, perhaps none more important than the dimensions of accountability occasioned by this step in the process. The Leadergroup now refers back to Step Two, and compares the results against the predetermined goals already defined. They can then decide to continue, revise or stop.

The decision to continue should now be based on the ability of the group to continue to meet the needs assessed above if the responses are, in themselves, adequately meeting those needs. Revision is a corrective action made at mid-stream or at this juncture according to the accomplishments of the group and the changes which may occur as it progresses. "Stop!" is always an alternative. But somehow, once certain things are placed on a budget, they seem to continue to be there indefinitely. It is always healthy to raise the question about whether or not what has "always been" should "always continue to be" in organizational life. Perhaps it is redundant to recognize that a Polytroph will not always be the most popular person at this point, especially if he is willing to look at the fatted cows on the budgets of ongoing institutions.

STEP SEVEN: REVISE AS REQUIRED.

This "step" may not be triggered sequentially, as mentioned above. It is not uncommon for situations to change, reflecting on changes in the initial needs assessment, which of course, impacts on the entire process from that point. While these occurrences can be considered an inconvenience, they can also become a profound learning experience when going through them, fostering greater wisdom, insight and skills in identifying future needs in a manner that takes into account other undiscovered contingencies.

Certainly, some changes will never be predictable, but will nevertheless impact the equations of change beyond our ability to control. These so-called "acts of God," such as death, economic collapse, political upheavals, physical calamities, and accidents, may be absolutely beyond even our most qualified and best intentioned control. When these things happen, it will be necessary to pick up the pieces from that point, re-evaluate the Needs Assessment, and go forward from there. A caring and responsive leader will always be prepared for change, and be sufficiently flexible to adapt in a manner consistent with the predetermined goals.

Notes

1. May, Rollo. *The Courage To Create*, New York: Bantam Books, 1975, p. 46.
2. Ibid.
3. Baird, Kenyon R. *The Willingness of Polytrophic and Authoritarian Leaders to Utilize a System Approach to Problem Solving.* (San Diego: Doctoral Dissertation; United States International University, 1977) Ann Arbor, MI: University Microfilm International, 1985.

CHAPTER ELEVEN

If You Love Me... Feed My Lambs, Shepherd My Sheep, and Feed My Sheep!

Agape love is a choice! *"God so loved this world that he gave his only begotten Son, so that anyone who believes in him should not perish but have everlasting life."* If we learn to love as God has loved us, then we too shall make choices to love others as well.

It seems obvious to a lover to scratch others where he itches. Unfortunately, the contemporary church has had a history of shooting its soldiers in the foot. Enormous pain has been inflicted on others by fellow Christians, unable to distinguish between justice and love. Nothing is quite as hard to explain as the behaviors of those who bear the name of Christ when their actions are diametrically opposed to the love which should identify His followers. While it remains true that the believer has the treasure of the Holy Spirit indwelling an "earthen vessel," and some people are more earthen than others in their behaviors, there seems to be a basic dissimilarity in belief and behavior.

The "carnal" Christian has been present since the early church. This phenomenon can best be understood in terms of spiritual immaturity. Paul spoke of those who were not ready for real spiritual meat because they were still infants who could only handle milk.

The root word for "hypocrite" comes from the ancient theatre. It was normal for one person in a travelling theatrical group to act out more than one role. In so doing, he would wear the mask of the part he was playing. The word for the person who wore the mask was "upokritos." The word came to refer to the person who is not what he represents himself to be. Psycho-sociologically, it still represents someone who masks his "real" persona by saying one thing and doing another. This behavior has been the bane of Christendom, because the casual observer does not know the difference between an infant Christian and a mature one. Mature ones are in fact rarely seen.

Still in another sense such behavior represents the outworking of a life of faith. We are unfinished business as long as we indwell this fleshly body. God is not through with us yet. And perhaps the greatest yearning for the believer is to find victory over the strivings of the flesh, over human temptations, while still being fully human. Paul commanded however, that **love** be without hypocrisy. (Rom.12:9)

An astute observer of human behavior can easily recognize the hypocrisy that exists in many fields of endeavor such as politics, business, advertising, finance, sport and education. Unfortunately, it has become the norm to have hidden agenda, while offering a pittance for socially redeeming programs affecting those injured and left in their wake. When hidden agenda are left unrecognized, all sorts of organizational games ensue. The organization or group says that it has a certain mission, but in reality does not pursue it because other tasks have become more attractive. This can happen just as well in the Christian organization and the local church as in the secular organization and role.

One inner city ethnic church decided that it wanted to develop a Bible college to meet the needs of its constituency and its immediate demographic area. It was a great and reasonable response to the obvious needs that were around them. However, when they started to form their institution, a curious thing happened. Those who were going to be teachers and leaders suddenly got caught up with the perceived status of academia, calling one another "dean," "professor," and whenever possible the honorific "doctor." Their curriculum reflected their orientation to scholastic status, offering classes named "Pedagogy I and II" rather than meeting the real needs of the community. Starting with the best of intentions, other temptations got in the way of simple servant-leadership. Their concern about meeting needs in their church and community soon became overshadowed by concerns about status. The Polytrophic leader, as an effective consultant, can create considerable benefit simply by identifying these concealed directives and thereby cutting the power to the organizational game.

But when it comes to loving, the Bible says that we should do **that** without hypocrisy!

So how does the contemporary Christian accomplish this?

Do you remember the Apostle Peter's reaction in the wake of the crucifixion? After the zenith of Christ's intervention into the motley band's lives, perhaps attempting to filter through the explosive events of the past weeks, but certainly blunted in their understanding of kingdom events, Peter makes the profound statement, "I'm going out to fish." Thomas, Nathanael, James and John all respond alike, "We'll go with you." (John 21:1-3)

They were not goofing off. These robust fishermen were returning to their old ways and means, their familiar nets, the old smells and callouses. This was the old life, based on heritage, environment, specific conditioning, values and choices. I sense in the brusque declaration of Peter, that the Lord's incredible intervention into their lives was much, much greater than they could ever have imagined, but now that He was taken from them (so they apparently believed) he "might as well" go back to the old rut. It was the "natural" thing to do.

Peter and the group were seemingly coping with their enormous but unspeakable disappointment in the best way they knew. The group derived a great deal of pleasure in the camaraderie of its male dominated fishing enterprise. Bear in mind that the old rut also provided a certain status, a modicum of financial power, and control over life's direction. That is, obviously, if it weren't for the Lord's penchant for lovingly interrupting our common ruts with the intervention of glaring failure in our trivial pursuits.... "that night they caught nothing." Sometimes He has other fish to fry!

John's gospel is poignant as it relates the account of the risen Lord asking Peter, "Do you truly love me more than these?" The "these" refers to his whole life of fishing, its status, leadership relationships, personal power, its enculturation of Peter, his sense of identity, security, mobility and role in this world. It was a deeply probing question to a person who was now aware of his own propensity for spontaneous screw-ups in spiritual matters. In a sense the Lord always probes his followers who inevitably encounter a never ending flow of "these" kinds of experiences and their attendant opportunities for idolatry. The Lord always demands that we keep clear our affection for Him.

There is a monumental word play on "love" that punches through the narrative. Jesus keeps using the word "agape," and Peter keeps responding with the word "phileo." Simply rendered, Jesus asks Peter if he loves him in the same manner in which God loves him, i.e., unashamedly, without reserve, unconditionally. The most that Peter can now respond is that he "likes" Jesus. The word that Peter selects to respond to Jesus is a profound confession of his human inability to perform any better than he has in the past. No more boasting. No more promises. No more expectations based on fervor rather than ability to produce appropriate results. When pressed by the risen Lord who repeats the question a third time, the now subdued Peter responds, "Lord, you know all things; you know that I like you." There is a humbling of the fisherman, a cleansing of the relationship, given the unique personality of Peter, in which Peter has now realized that his brusque leadership posturing for the benefit of the others around him, his playing to the crowd with its disastrous consequences, no longer will be offered, expected, or tolerated.

Also, while Peter softly admits that he can see himself giving only what he has, that is, to the level of his insight and ability, the Lord assures him that such a basis is an acceptable foundation on which to build and go forward. He reinforces Peter with a pronouncement of how events will work out in Peter's life now that Peter has finally learned what Lordship, love, and real life is based on. Then Jesus affirms him with the task, "Follow Me!" When Peter's thinking wanders off track immediately in his concern about John, Christ is quick to correct and affirm, "What's that to you? You must follow me." It is a marvelous account of the Lord penetrating a personality in the most forceful way so that the person learns priorities, and with the right priorities, the right motives. Peter is on the road of discovering that love is a choice made by a mature person concerned about eternal values. This is authenticity!

Undoubtedly, Peter's confession also stimulated him to gather that he could only do so much in his own personal power and human strength. The warm supportive response by the Lord Jesus also promised that Peter would one day be empowered by the Holy Spirit, enabling him to function on a supernatural level of human experience. Perhaps these pristine illustrations of Peter in the Bible account for his affectionate appreciation by all subsequent believers, because every person may take great solace in both Peter's desperate human blunders, and the Lord's enabling grace. Knowing deeply our own formidable bent to sin, how good to realize that there is hope in Christ not only to forgive and redirect, but to empower us to live appropriate lives in contemporary society.

Agape love is never passive. The polytrophic person makes the choice to love and gets involved; intelligently and with wisdom. An astute agape-lover will be sensitive to all sorts of the needs which ultimately stem from spiritual destitution. He recognizes that there are millions of people without Christ as Lord and Saviour. He also realizes that those who name Him fall far short of maturity.

Some years ago a classic book appeared called *The Incendiary Fellowship* in which the author, Elton Trueblood, cited the principle that it was God's program to work through the local church. In a similar fashion, it appears that God will work through his own people who love to reach a world estranged from Him. Christians ARE the salt of the earth. Certainly they can lose their saltiness, but they do have the ability to do the Lord's work in the Lord's way, i.e., through love.

Jesus gave a powerful indictment of the Jews as recorded in John's gospel. (Jn 5:39ff) He said, *"You do not have the love of God within you."* This was directed to those who searched the scriptures, believing that in them they had eternal life. Such an indictment is still viable for the contemporary church whenever it gets caught up in matters of status, power and control. In the same passage Jesus asks, *"How can you believe, who receive glory from one another and do not seek the glory that comes from the only God?"*

In John's letter, he makes a clear, simple, and at once profound statement,

> *Beloved, let us love one another; for love is of God, and he who loves is born of God and knows God. He who does not love does not know God; for God is love.*

Matthew recounts what Jesus said about his return in all his glory with the angels, to sit on his glorious throne:

> *'Come, O blessed of my Father, inherit the kingdom prepared for you from the foundation of the world; for I was hungry and you gave me food, I was thirsty and you gave me drink, I was a stranger and you welcomed me, I was naked and you clothed me, I was sick and you visited me, I was in prison and you came to me.' Then the righteous will answer him, 'Lord, when did we see you hungry and feed you, or thirsty and give you drink? And when did we see you a stranger and welcome you, or naked and clothe you? And when did we see you sick or in prison and visit you?' And the King shall answer them, 'Truly, I say to you, as you did it to one of the least of these my brethren, you did it to me.'*

Recently, a disturbing and enlightening book entitled Target Earth was co-published by the University of the Nations in Kailua-Kona, Hawaii, and Global Mapping International, Pasadena, California. The jacket cover carries these statements:

> This atlas presents graphic reality ... it presents an invitation to participate in the final assault on the powers of darkness, employing all the mammoth resources now at your disposal—not the least of which is this superb atlas.
>
> This book, as presented with facts and maps and with some 50 contributors from many vocations and walks of Christian life, is in itself a testimony of its message: It is the body of Christ, diversified in talent and calling, working together to complete the Great Commission and living according to the Great Commandment.

In both graphic depiction and relevant prose, the "Atlas" gives some startling information coupled with Biblical directives. Notice a few examples:

> Seventy million people are on the threshold of starvation (another 400 million consume less than "the minimum critical diet" according to the World Bank). Eight hundred million live in absolute poverty. Half of the children in this category will not survive until their fifth birthday. Of the 800 million in absolute poverty, 195 million are our brothers and sisters in Christ. There is something desperately wrong in the body of Christ when some of us are living palatially and others starve to death.
>
> A quarter of a million children die each week from frequent infections and prolonged undernutrition. Of those children who do not die, ill-health and poor growth are common, thus restricting their full mental and physical development. It is now possible to prevent most childhood deaths and malnutrition using means which developing nations can afford. In a difficult economic climate with limited promotion of low-cost means for protecting children, 14,000 young lives are saved each week. How? By informing and supporting parents in basic and inexpensive actions such as: immunizing their children, using oral rehydration therapies (ORT), maintaining

exclusive breast feeding in the early months, training when and how to introduce other foods, recognizing danger signs of acute respiratory infection, spacing births at least two years apart,and finally, by practicing prenatal care and home hygiene. When fully applied, these low-cost techniques could reduce child mortality by 125,000 per week. Such programs can and must be supported by every nation.

The Word of God has much to say about poverty, prosperity, and care of the poor and needy. Our involvement requires both head and heart. We need to do research and educate ourselves on the nature of this problem, to pray for God's mercy, intervention and revealed wisdom, and to properly apply Biblical truth to every facet of this crisis.

Our involvement must also include intervention with the poor and needy. Healthcare, education, and economic development are required to address physical and emotional needs, evangelism and church planting to address spiritual needs.

Christian involvement must also take place at policy/decision making level. The world is waiting for the Daniels, Josephs, and Solomons of our generation to arise and take their place in the affairs of the nations.

A recent occurrence in the sportsworld illustrates a similar problem in contemporary Christendom. It seems that a major league baseball club, seemingly loaded with talent, continues to play far below its anticipated standards of accomplishments. After rousing team meetings the players go out and play competitively for a few games, establish a winning record, than slide back into the losing doldroms again. Now they have concluded that they must play each and every game as though it is the most important game of the year for them. And they are!

The problems which occur in our churches and Christian organizations are not necessarily happening because of a lack of knowledge or insight, although we can always learn more and become better equipped. Perhaps it is an issue both of priorities and the willingness to make the choice to love. To do what we are supposed to be doing!

We have explored the reasons why certain people grow in certain ways, relationships between leader styles and follower needs, steps to organizational growth, and explored the basic framework for the kinds of sin which alienate. This can become simply another book in the long weariness of bookmaking unless you, the aspiring leader, not only make the right choices to love, but simply go ahead and DO something about the needs around you. Look at your own life. Your family relationships. Your church. Your sense of stewardship in all of life's responsibilities and opportunities. Start with your own needs assessment ... and get about the work that God has for you. Prayerfully consider "What Should Be" and seek His guidance as you creatively develop options and alternatives for the stewardship of your life. And may the Lord grant you the courage and wisdom to implement whatever He leads you into.

May the joy of God's love consume you as you respond to contemporary needs in this, God's world of opportunity.